TABLE OF CONTENTS

Top 20 Test Taking Tips

1. Carefully follow all the test registration procedures
2. Know the test directions, duration, topics, question types, how many questions
3. Setup a flexible study schedule at least 3-4 weeks before test day
4. Study during the time of day you are most alert, relaxed, and stress free
5. Maximize your learning style; visual learner use visual study aids, auditory learner use auditory study aids
6. Focus on your weakest knowledge base
7. Find a study partner to review with and help clarify questions
8. Practice, practice, practice
9. Get a good night's sleep; don't try to cram the night before the test
10. Eat a well balanced meal
11. Know the exact physical location of the testing site; drive the route to the site prior to test day
12. Bring a set of ear plugs; the testing center could be noisy
13. Wear comfortable, loose fitting, layered clothing to the testing center; prepare for it to be either cold or hot during the test
14. Bring at least 2 current forms of ID to the testing center
15. Arrive to the test early; be prepared to wait and be patient
16. Eliminate the obviously wrong answer choices, then guess the first remaining choice
17. Pace yourself; don't rush, but keep working and move on if you get stuck
18. Maintain a positive attitude even if the test is going poorly
19. Keep your first answer unless you are positive it is wrong
20. Check your work, don't make a careless mistake

Internal/Management Control

Internal control objectives

The purposes of internal controls are:

Put in place in order to achieve stated corporate goals.

Provide management with a way in which the progress toward stated goals can be monitored.

Ensure that corporate resources are utilized in a proper and efficient manner and are not being used in an unauthorized or inappropriate manner.

Allows management to make necessary changes to a particular internal control if it is found that control is inefficient or irrelevant.

To ensure that all transactions are properly documented which helps to ensure that all performance, financial and other reporting is accurate and up to date.

To ensure that all employees are adhering to applicable laws, rules and regulations.

Information and communications

Information and communications controls are put in place to ensure that information is reported accurately and in a timely fashion to the necessary departments. This information is necessary for internal as well as external uses. The efficient and timely reporting of information is necessary in order to comply with activities such as external financial reporting to various government agencies. Internally, the importance of reporting information accurately and in a timely manner can refer to such activities such as the acquisition of equipment and fixed assets, budgeting, the reporting of receivables and payables and inventories. Effectively and accurately communicating information is of significant importance toward achieving corporate goals. Information that is not reported in a timely manner or is reported erroneously has the potential of having a significant negative impact on the corporation.

Financial management principles

The three major principles of Financial Management and Control according to the GAO:

Adherence to laws, rules and regulations as they specifically apply to the corporation.

Ensuring that all financial reporting including budgets and earnings forecasts and all other financial statements, whether for internal or external use are trustworthy, truthful and reliable. Corporate resources are being utilized in a manner that is effective as well as efficient and ethical. By adhering to these major principles, management teams use internal controls as a system of checks and balances in order to meet the corporations' overall objectives. While implementing an internal controls system, management should perform a cost/benefit analysis and critically evaluate outside factors that may determine the efficiency of such controls. Finally, although internal controls may help instill confidence toward the attainment of corporate goals, they are not a guarantee that those goals will be met.

Internal control considerations

Risk assessment

All internal and external risks should be assessed clearly and objectively in conjunction with corporate goals. Once risk is identified, management should determine how to mitigate and manage risk. Due to fluctuations and changes in economies, markets, regulations and general operating conditions, guidelines should be set in place as to how to best deal with such factors. Risk assessments used may vary, but should include both qualitative and quantitative methods whenever possible as well as, analyses through budget and earnings forecasting, audits and other financial reporting.

Once risks are assessed and their severity and likelihood of occurring is determined, careful planning should be utilized when attempting to hedge those risks.

One of the first steps in assessing risk is to make sure that the level of acceptable risk. The definition of necessary risk and the policies and procedures for mitigating those risks are properly and effectively communicated to all necessary personnel. Managers should also evaluate employees to ensure adherence to those guidelines. In order to monitor and stay abreast of risks, corporations should continually evaluate the initial guidelines put in place to manage risk. The efficacy and relevance of those guidelines should be determined and the appropriate changes to guidelines should be made when deemed necessary. Once risks have been determined, careful consideration should be utilized when preparing a plan for necessary actions to lessen or mitigate those risks. Other considerations that should be taken into account are changes in the overall corporate environment such as expansion and growth or restructuring and downsizing.

Limitations in risk assessment arise when the internal control objectives are not adequately being met. Matters that are of a subjective nature can present limitations due to errors in judgment and miscalculation when evaluating risk. Risk assessment is limited if the information it is based on is faulty or unreliable. Mistakes made through technological breakdowns or human error also limits effective risk assessment. When basic internal control objectives are not being met, this can lead to a breakdown in many areas and departments. For example, risk assessment would not be accurate in cases of unethical or unlawful behavior by any person or persons employed with the corporation. The most basic reasons behind implementing internal controls to achieving corporate goals with the reasonable assurance that it is being done so while adhering to applicable local and federal laws and regulations. This behavior could not only negate many different areas of internal controls but also negate the basic reasons internal controls are put into action.

There are many *inherent risks* pertaining to internal controls due to the fact that internal control encompasses the activities, personalities and behaviors of the entire staff, management and executives of a corporation or federal agency as a whole. There are both internal and external inherent risks that may prevent the success of internal controls, thereby, hindering the goals and objectives of the corporation or federal agency. In order to mitigate these inherent risks, management should clearly and effectively state expected behaviors, performance and duties of the corporations' staff, management and executives. Communicating the consequences of illegal, inappropriate and unacceptable activities and behaviors may also mitigate inherent risk. At its' most basic, inherent risk is always present due to the differing morals, values, character and personalities of the staff, management and executives employed by the corporation or federal agency.

Assessing risk controls

Corporate objectives – All corporate goals should be clearly dictated and communicated with all employees. Corporate goals should be attainable and specific steps toward the attainment of those goals should be dictated clearly. Departmental management should be provided with the opportunity to offer feedback regarding the attainability of stated goals as they pertain to their respective departments. When developing a plan toward the achievement of corporate goals, management must adhere to all Federal and local laws, rules and regulations. While establishing corporate goals, internal as well as external risk factors should be taken into consideration and sufficient measures to mitigate risks should be taken whenever possible. Finally, all strategies regarding corporate goals and objectives should take into consideration past performance and proper asset allocation.

Activity level objectives – Once the overall corporate objectives are communicated, the activity level toward the achievement of attaining corporate goals should be reviewed. A review of activities helps to ensure that they remain relevant and offers management the ability to make changes when necessary. It is important the activities related to corporate goals are in sync with each other and are not working against one another. It is also important that the proper amount of resources have been allocated to the appropriate departments in order to successfully complete necessary activities toward the achievement of corporate goals. If it is found that there is a shortage of resources, then a plan should be devised in order to compensate for the shortages. Finally, activities should be ranked by order of critical importance toward the achievement of corporate goals and objectives.

Risk identification – Identifying risks should be done so by using both qualitative and quantitative measures and should be ranked by order of importance or significance and whether or not they are long or short-term risks. Plans should be implemented in order to mitigate identified risks as much as possible. Appropriate levels of risk should be clearly communicated and acknowledged to all necessary employees.

It is important for management to consider both external and internal risks as well as tangible and intangible risk.

- Examples of external risks may be economic climate, political unrest, advances in technologies, natural disaster or problems that occur with outside suppliers and contractors.
- Examples of internal risks may be incompetence of employees, not offering competitive salaries or benefits plans and inadequate safeguarding of assets and information.

Risk analysis -- Once identified, it is important for management to make a critical analysis of those risks and the effects they may have on the achievement of corporate goals. This can be done by first establishing a ranking order of the identified risks.

- Those falling into the high-risk category should be dealt with first.
- During the analysis management should determine the probability of each risk occurring and how often the risk is likely to occur.
- Once this analysis is made, a plan should be put in to place in order to lessen the severity of any negative impact the risks may have on the corporation.
- Finally, it should be clearly determined the level of acceptable risk the corporation is willing to take on.

These levels should be clearly communicated to and understood by, all employees.

Managing risk during change – Although external change cannot be predicted, it is important that management anticipate change and measures are put in place in order to handle these changes. Ways to anticipate external changes may be:

- Keeping abreast of economic conditions and forecasts
- Existing and proposed governmental regulations and laws industry
- Wide performances and political climates.

Just as with other risk analyses, these actual and anticipated changes should be ranked by level of importance and those that have or will have the most significant impact on the corporation should be dealt with first. Some examples of more significant changes are high levels of employee turnover, new laws or regulations that significantly change the course of daily business activities, the possibility of downsizing due to loss of profits or decreased demand or cases of rapid growth or expansion.

General application of control activities – In order for control activities to be considered effective, management must clearly communicate the appropriate policies and procedures to all employees. Once communicated, confirmation that all employees understand these policies and procedures should be obtained. This confirmation is often obtained by having the employee sign the relevant manual such as a policy and procedures manual or employee handbook. All control activities should be periodically evaluated in order to determine whether or not they remain relevant and efficient. If it is found that the activity is no longer relevant then it should be discontinued or changed. If it is found that a control activity does not make efficient use of time or resources, it should be brought to the attention of management and the appropriate changes should be implemented.

Cost-benefit considerations

Cost benefit considerations are necessary for evaluating the efficiency and relevancy of an internal control. For example, if a certain department is experiencing a large number of errors or has an unusually high attrition rate, management should review the human resources controls for that department. This could include amending hiring standards and training programs. It may benefit the company to incorporate a longer or more in-depth training program to ensure that the employee's for that department are receiving all of the pertinent information and the appropriate training in order to perform their job duties more effectively and efficiently. In this case, the benefit of improving the training program would outweigh the associated costs. Cost benefit considerations are also helpful when attempting to determine whether or not a control activity remains relevant. For example, in the case of advances in technology, cost-benefit considerations should be evaluated when determining whether or not to purchase new equipment to replace duties that have been performed manually.

Ineffective cost-benefit analysis

Cost benefit analysis often relies on quantifiable and tangible data. In all corporations there are matters that are intangible and therefore cannot be quantified or measured. Areas where a traditional cost benefit analysis may be difficult or ineffective are often of a subjective nature such as employee morale or public perception of the company. For instance, although employee morale cannot be physically measured, it can have a significant impact on the overall goals of the corporation. If morale is low due to lay-offs, budget cuts effecting employee benefits or pay freezes, employee production drops and revenue decreases. Management would have to perform a cost benefit analysis applying subjective judgment rather than physical data. This same subjective judgment would also be applied in issues of public perception.

Cost-benefit analysis framework

The basic framework when analyzing costs should include, but is not limited to, the following:

- Determining and outlining corporate goals.
- Defining a plan toward the achievement of those goals.
- Defining related costs.
- Breaking down costs into categories of ongoing or constant costs or one-time costs.
- Determining the cost to maintain a program, activity or equipment.
- Determining production costs.
- Determining opportunity cost. That is to say, if the company invested its' money elsewhere, would the rate of return be higher in the long-term and therefore more beneficial for the corporation.
- In depth evaluation of what costs would be in the case of failure.
- These costs should then be weighed against the benefits. The basic framework when analyzing benefits should include, but is not limited to, the following:
- Determining whether or not the benefits are ongoing or one-time benefits.
- Determining whether revenue will increase.
- Determining whether labor cost will decrease.
- Determining how risk is affected and whether or not risk is increased or decreased.

- Determining the effect of intangibles such as increased or decreased employee morale and public perception.

Material weaknesses

Material weaknesses occur when there is a significant breakdown in internal controls regarding financial reporting. When management initially puts into place internal controls regarding financial reporting, it must be effectively communicated to employees. Management should monitor those employees to ensure that they are complying with internal control guidelines on a consistent basis. If communication of those controls is not complete it becomes ineffective and that can lead to varying methods of financial inputs that, in turn, may lead to inconsistencies in financial reporting. Not all breakdowns in internal controls are significant enough to be considered a material weakness. Auditors should take great care when evaluating whether or not a breakdown should be considered significant based on the following criteria: the frequency of occurrence, the likelihood of reoccurrence and the overall impact the breakdown has.

Internal control applications

Control environment

The control environment relates to the intangible environment of a corporation such as employee outlook and morale as well as corporate philosophies and mission statements. The control environment also relates to management style, how management relays its' philosophies and corporate goals to employee's and the effect management style has on employee's. Control environments can be effected negatively or positively depending on the tone set by management. Management also affects employees' directly by their behavior. For example, if management is found to be consistently unethical, then employees' may follow their lead and think it acceptable to behave unethically as well. If management leads by example by behaving ethically and professionally, then employees will more than likely follow their positive lead.

Control activities

Control activities relate to the policy and procedures manuals and employee behavior guidelines as defined by upper management and top executives. These manuals and guidelines are utilized to ensure that employees and management are adhering to the expected standards and practices of the corporation. These guidelines should be provided to help make certain that management direction is being properly carried out and ethical practices and standards are being met.

Control Activities encompass all levels of the corporation and include such things as *recording data accurately and in a timely manner, establishing guidelines for performance reviews, the proper performance of expected duties and managing human resources as well as other corporate capital.*

Control Activities as they relate to human resource management should encompass hiring and employing personnel that properly fit job descriptions and providing proper training and incentives for those personnel. Employee retention and success should also be fostered in order to achieve and maintain a low attrition rate and achieve corporate objectives.

Assessing control activities:

Human resources – Reviews are necessary in order to ensure that the corporation federal agency is progressing toward, and meeting its' stated goals. Reviews are also used as a way to determine whether or not an employee is performing his or her duties adequately. Human resource management controls are necessary in order to ensure that well qualified candidates are being hired and can fully carry out their expected job duties. Developing and conducting an adequate and thorough employee-training program is necessary to ensure employee success in job performance. Developing a comprehensive employee handbook and policies and procedures manual helps to ensure that all employees adhere to expected corporate and agency standards. Federal agencies and corporations should be sure that adequate training of human resource employees regarding issues such as pay, benefits and grievances is conducted so that those matters are handled properly. This may include a comprehensive review of laws and regulations such as The EOE Act, Sarbanes-Oxley and OSHA standards. Clear separation of authority and assigned duties avoids confusion among employees regarding to whom they are to report. Separation of duties is also necessary in order to have a clear definition of what is expected from employees and managers

Specific policies should be in place regarding human resources management. This includes the hiring and training process as well as measure to be taken when dealing with problems such as grievances and issues such as benefits, pay structure, promotions, disciplinary actions and termination. All relevant employee issues should be effectively communicated with the proper upper level management personnel. All employees should receive the proper level of supervision and guidance by their superiors. It is also important that all persons employed in a management capacity possess adequate skill sets in order to successfully and effectively manage the different personalities and needs of their respective subordinates as well as, the ability to effectively communicate to upper level management regarding any issues within their respective departments.

Over Information and Technology:

- *Information processing management:* information processing controls are important in order to make certain that information from transactions is being recorded properly, accurately and in a timely fashion. These controls may include providing employee passwords in order to ensure that unauthorized use of the information systems does not occur.
- *Maintenance of information and technology systems:* Information and technology systems must be maintained in order to prevent breaches in security of sensitive information or losses of information due to system breakdowns. Controls over maintenance of information and technology systems should include contingencies for system failure and adequate system security such as firewalls to protect the data contained within the system. Regular maintenance of system hardware should also be performed regularly in order to check for signs of deterioration.

Business and behavioral ethics – Corporations must establish an expected code of conduct for all employees, including executives and upper level management. This code of conduct should be properly communicated and acknowledged by all employees. Penalties and disciplinary action taken for failures to adhere to ethical guidelines should also be clearly communicated and acknowledged.

All interactions with outside parties such as suppliers and regulatory bodies should be conducted according to the same code of ethics. Employees should offer full disclosure when dealing with regulatory bodies and auditors and all information should be truthful and reliable. All mistakes made in billing to or from suppliers and customers should be corrected in a timely fashion. If it is found that an employee has breached the established code of ethical conduct, the appropriate personnel should deal with the issue in a fair and timely manner.

Competence -- Human resources controls should be developed and implemented in order to ensure that only the most qualified applicants are selected for hire. Complete and accurate job descriptions should also be communicated and understood by management and employees. Corporations should provide proper and adequate training programs for new hires as well as, continual training for existing employees.
Continual training helps to provide employees with the most up to date materials in order to help them to improve and maintain a high level of competence regarding job performance. It is also important that the trainers and managers of training programs possess the necessary skills to train and advise employees properly and successfully.

Management Philosophy and Operating Style – Management philosophies should be clearly communicated and understood by all employees and the operating style should contribute to a positive and supportive environment. A key factor when assessing whether or not internal controls over management is effective is employee turnover or attrition. If a high turnover rate of employees' exists, this is indicative of internal control failures in one or many departments. Once this failure is discovered, corrective measures should be taken. Lines of communication for all levels of management should remain open; this helps to foster a positive and cohesive corporate environment as well as, quick resolution when problems arise. Finally, all reports submitted should be accurate, reliable and truthful.

Organizational Structure – When establishing an organizational structure it is important for management to evaluate the needs of the corporation to be sure that the organizational structure is appropriate and adequate. All employees should be aware of their duties and responsibilities and lines of communication between management and staff should remain open. The organizational structure should be evaluated from time to time in order to adjust for changes in the corporate environment or other outside factors such as changes in economies, supply or demand. Finally, management should be sure that all departments have a sufficient amount of employees in order to complete job requirements. When employee shortages occur, there may be an increased level of mistakes made due to the increased workload.

Oversight Groups – Oversight groups are necessary in order to monitor activities and business transactions within the corporation. It is common that an outside party such as an Inspector General, whom has no direct association with the corporation, conduct management reviews and audits. This ensures that there are no instances of conflicts of interest or bias. When appropriate, an audit committee is formed so that internal and external auditors may work together regarding reviews and audits. It is important that corporate officials respect and cooperate with regulatory agencies such as the OMB, SEC, GAO and the Department of Treasury. Finally, all necessary reports to regulatory agencies such as the ones mentioned are filed in a timely manner and contain accurate, reliable and truthful information.

Monitoring activities

Monitoring activities are necessary in order to evaluate and ensure activities and duties are carried out as specified by management. Monitoring is also used to evaluate financial performance through audits to ensure compliance with laws and regulations.

Audits can be performed internally, externally or both. Audits are also necessary in order to evaluate progress toward achieving corporate goals.

Monitoring activities also involve employee reviews in order to evaluate an employees' performance as well as, determine strengths and weaknesses as they pertain to his or her job duties. Strengths should be recognized and weaknesses should be carefully evaluated. After weaknesses are identified, a clear plan of action should be discussed and implemented in order to improve upon and correct those weaknesses. Any serious deficiencies in performance or findings of employee incompetence should be promptly reported to upper management.

Compensating controls

Compensating controls may be necessary for corporations in which there is not enough staff or resources available in order to establish a clear separation of expected duties. The separation of duties is an integral component of the internal control system and its' successful implementation. The inability to establish a separation of duties resulting in the implementation of compensating controls may expose the corporation up to increased business risk. Compensating controls may also be necessary in cases of material weakness or when less significant control weaknesses exist. The implementation of these controls may be necessary in order to compensate for the existing ineffective aspects of the current internal controls in place.

General control activities

General Control refers to all information technology systems, including all application software, databases, mainframes, networks and end-users. General controls are utilized to manage computer security systems as well as, the management of information that is entered and stored within the corporations' mainframes and databases. Guidelines should be provided regarding system backups and recovery of information in the case of system failure. General Controls are also necessary to protect the overall information system from corruption through illegal or unauthorized use resulting from hackers or inappropriate use by employees. Examples of General Control activities may include frequently changing passwords, varying dial-up numbers on a regular basis, allowing employee's access to only the information necessary to perform their specific duties and the prompt deactivation of passwords for employees that have left the corporation.

Application control

Application Controls specific to information systems as dictated by the GAO are developed and implemented in order to make sure that all data entering and exiting the systems are accurate and reliable.

- Application controls are also necessary to ensure that only authorized user's access restricted or confidential information and perform data inputs and outputs.
- Application controls help to ensure that all transactions made within information technology systems are valid and not the product of fraud or illegal activities.
- The efficacy of application control is dependent upon how successfully the general controls over information systems are implemented.
- Finally, information technology application controls must possess a level of flexibility due to the rapid changes and advancements in the overall technology market.

Internal controls responsibilities

Auditors:

- Auditors' main responsibilities are to objectively evaluate the overall internal control environment.
- After the environment is adequately evaluated, auditors should then make suggestions to management for ways to strengthen internal control when necessary and/or to eliminate controls that have become obsolete or irrelevant.
- Additional responsibilities include making sure that all financial paperwork, such as taxes or required SEC documents, is filed in a timely manner and that the information contained in the reports is accurate and reliable.
- Auditors' responsibilities also include reviewing legal issues that may affect corporate finances as well as investigating and detecting possible instances of fraudulent activities such as embezzlement.
- During the course of an investigation in cases of possible fraudulent activities, auditors should be sure to conduct thorough interviews as well as, investigate business transactions that are both financial and non-financial.

Management – The environment of the corporation as well as its' internal controls should be exhibited in manner that is both positive and well organized. This includes maintaining ethical standards and integrity by all employees. Management should clearly dictate what is considered unethical or improper behavior and provide the proper level of discipline when necessary. The corporate hierarchal structure should also be clearly defined; this includes the delegation of authority. A clear delineation of authority prevents confusion regarding reporting, responsibility and conflict. It is important for management to develop standard practices of hiring, as well as, proper and sufficient training programs. This ensures that a prospective employees' skill set is properly matched with his or her duties and that those duties are carried out in a competent and efficient manner. Finally, management should offer constructive criticism and support as well as maintain a high level of professionalism when communicating with government oversight agencies and committees.

Employees and other personnel – Although management and upper executives often define internal controls and are ultimately responsible for the successes and failures of those controls, it is the responsibility of the entire corporation to ensure that internal controls in place are adhered to and upheld. It is the responsibility of all employees to report unethical and unlawful behavior or violations of laws and regulations to the proper personnel. Another example of employee responsibility to internal controls is that each employee is expected to perform their job duties and tasks to the best of their abilities and to complete continuing professional education and training programs as necessary.

Corporate objectives and goals cannot be successfully attained without the participation and cooperation of all those employed within the corporation.

Establishing internal controls

Once the corporations' main goals have been established, management must then develop internal controls for the achievement of those corporate goals. These internal controls are necessary not only in corporate goal achievement, but to also to help ensure that the corporation is operating in an organized and cost effective manner. These internal controls help to diffuse any confusion regarding the responsibilities of individual employees and departments. Management must decide the following when establishing internal controls: where internal controls are necessary and documenting the components that make up the internal control. Management should take care to establish specific internal controls as they apply to specific departments. These internal controls should be communicated with all departments and employees.

Once management has established the internal controls, it is important that those internal controls are maintained. This is done by continually reviewing internal controls in order to determine whether or not they remain relevant and effective. Different types of reviews may include interviews with employees and/or department heads and conducting analyses of the overall control environment. This gives management the opportunity to monitor changes in the external environment that may affect the corporation such as changes in the state of the national economy, changes in supply and demand, technological advances and legal and regulatory changes. Any of these external factors may significantly affect the efficiency of current internal controls. By continually monitoring internal controls, management can keep up to date with all changes and adjust internal controls as the situation dictates.

Periodic reporting

Periodic reporting on internal controls is necessary to not only evaluate whether or not internal controls are adequate but to develop a plan of improvement for internal controls that are found to be inadequate during the evaluation phase. Management reports on internal controls should be given to all relevant personnel in order to better achieve corporate goals. The 3 main purposes for management reporting on internal controls are:

- To determine the overall condition of the internal controls
- To develop and plan any corrective actions for material weaknesses or deficiencies
- To evaluate the progress of those plans.

Management reports should also include all necessary requirements that are dictated by applicable laws and regulations such as the Federal Managers Financial Integrity Act.

Components of internal controls

Common control activities

Categories – Reviews are an important control activity and should be conducted at all corporate levels in order to determine the relevance and efficiency of internal controls.

- At the top-level, reviews of the overall corporate performance as well as budgets and forecasts should be conducted and long-term plans should be developed.

- Reviews at management and other levels should be conducted in order to determine whether or not activities are on track to meet corporate goals.

- Standard performance measurements should be developed and utilized in order to determine corporate successes and failures.

- Another common control activity involves human resource management. This includes hiring, training and termination procedures as well as promotions, benefits, salaries, job descriptions and incentives offered.

- Controls should also be in place to monitor information processing to ensure that data is properly and accurately documented. This also ensures that access to sensitive data is controlled and authorized.

- Controls over assets should be in place so that all assets are safeguarded and to help prevent instances of fraud or collusion.

- Finally, responsibilities of employees and management should be clearly stated.

As they pertain to the general control over information systems – General controls are in place in order to manage the information systems over the entire corporation. One of the first controls in place should involve the security of the information systems. It is important for management to assess the risk of breaches of security or loss of sensitive data. Polices and procedures involving corporate data should be clearly communicated to all employees. Given how quickly technology advances, security programs should be evaluated as often as necessary and any weaknesses found should be corrected at that time. It is also important that controls are in place that clearly authorized users of classified or sensitive information and steps should be taken in order to prevent unauthorized access. If unauthorized access should occur, procedures should be in place regarding how that situation is to be dealt with and what disciplinary actions are to be taken.

As they pertain to application and system software – All system software changes, updates, improvements or purchases of new software should be handled by the appropriate personnel and tested for efficacy before being put into general use. All changes made to Application and system software should also be carefully monitored. Monitoring these changes helps to ensure that unnecessary changes or not made and that all changes or improvements made are beneficial to the corporation. All software licensed to and/or owned by the corporation should be properly cataloged and labeled. Controls should be in place regarding the access to corporate software. All access to application and system software should be monitored; this helps to prevent unnecessary or unauthorized access.

Over segregation of duties -- It is important that all employees are hired for jobs that match their skill sets:

- Human resources controls should be in place to ensure that this occurs. This includes the proper hiring and training of new employees.
- Corporate wide, it is important to develop and clearly communicate the job descriptions and duties of each position.
- Once duties have been clearly defined and segregated, it is important that upper level management enforces those roles. This helps to prevent confusion among departments and employees as to corporate hierarchy and the expected roles and responsibilities of each department.
- Finally, controls should be in place regarding adequate supervision and departmental and employee reviews.

As they pertain to service continuity – All electronic data, software and equipment should be prioritized by level of importance, depending upon sensitivity and critical criteria:

- All software and information systems should be checked for wear, damage and/or corruption, in order to prevent potentially damaging and debilitating system failures or service interruptions.
- All personnel and staff should be properly trained in the procedures to be taken for the maintenance, back up and repair of the information systems.
- Upper level management should have a comprehensive plan in place in case a system failure event should occur and these back up plans should be tested as necessary in order to ensure that they will operate adequately until normal systems are operational.

Transactions within the computerized systems of the corporation:

- Adequate controls should be in place regarding access and authorization of source documents and periodic reviews and audits should be conducted in order to prevent and detect abuse or unauthorized use of source documents.
- Controls should also be in place to ensure that all source documents are accounted for.
- To further prevent corruption or misuse, access to data terminals where sensitive items such as source documents or master documents are stored should be adequately monitored and restricted to only necessary personnel.
- All transactions should be reconciled and verified in order to maintain accuracy and for verification purposes. This helps to prevent fraud and misuse as well as detect and correct errors in a timely manner.
- Finally, controls should be in place to ensure that the proper programs are being utilized for all transactions.

Information – All internal data should be accurate and reliable and should contain information relevant to corporate goals and objectives. All external information should also include data relevant to applicable laws, rules and regulations. The appropriate personnel should receive all relevant information in a timely manner and all information should contain adequate details in order for necessary tasks to be carried out. All financial statements and reports should adhere to all laws, rules and regulations and be filed with the appropriate regulatory bodies within the given time frame. Receiving accurate and reliable information in a timely manner is very important. This gives upper level management time to correct misstatements, to review that all information is accurate and/or to address any problems that are found to exist.

Communications – It is important that lines of communication remain open and clear at all levels of the corporate hierarchy. Top management must make clear what is expected of staff and job duties should be clearly stated and understood at all levels. Employees should also be offered alternatives in reporting other than exclusively to their direct superior. It should also be made apparent that negative information reported will not be met with retaliation or reprisal. Open lines of communication should not be restricted to internal operations but should include external operations as well. The corporation should communicate effectively and honestly with all outside agencies. Recommendations of outside agencies toward improvement in material deficiencies or weaknesses should be discussed and carefully considered by the appropriate personnel.

Means of communication – In dealing with the multitude of personalities in any corporation, some employees may not feel as comfortable communicating in person, especially if a problem exists. Corporations should offer differing forms of communication to help alleviate this problem. Offering different forms of communication such as e-mail and corporate wide intranets may also save time and resources. In order to ensure the success of electronic forms of communication, the corporate information system should be periodically evaluated and monitored in order to ensure that the systems remain relevant and effective. Periodic monitoring of information systems will aid in fixing any problems before those problems become compounded.

Ongoing monitoring – Ongoing monitoring is an important tool for management not only to assess progress toward corporate goals but also to identify existing and potential problems. If problems are found to exist, they should be carefully appraised through a separate evaluation. Ongoing monitoring also allows for management to assess the successes and failures in internal controls. Some common activities regarding ongoing monitoring are receiving feedback from employees through meetings and reports, developing a system that ensures that all information given and received is accurate and reliable. Developing such systems also helps to prevent fraud and/or collusion. Ongoing monitoring activities should also be developed regarding physical assets such as inventories, real property and other tangible assets. These activities ensure that there are no discrepancies between stated and actual assets.

Separate evaluations – Separate evaluations are important to ensure that internal controls remain effective and appropriate. Management should determine the methods used and frequency of such evaluations dependant upon the activity that is being evaluated. External factors such as economic conditions, technological advances and regulatory changes may affect the frequency of separate evaluations. Some examples of separate evaluations activities are employee and management self-assessments and comprehensive reviews of computer systems and corporate intranets. A common control activity regarding separate evaluations made by the Inspector general include ensuring that the Inspector General is provided with an adequate amount of resources in order to conduct the evaluation thoroughly and efficiently. There should also be a plan of action developed for reporting deficiencies or failures of internal controls discovered by the Inspector General.

Audit resolution – If material deficiencies or failures of internal controls are found during the course of an audit, a plan should be developed and implemented in order to resolve these negative findings in an appropriate and timely fashion. Once management and upper level executives discuss these negative findings, a plan of action should be developed toward the correction material deficiencies and weaknesses. If necessary, management should consult with regulatory bodies such as the GAO when difficulties arise regarding finding the appropriate path toward resolution and corrective actions for discovered material weaknesses and deficiencies. Once the corrective actions have been determined and implemented and audit follow up should be conducted to appraise the success of the corrective actions.

Evaluation process

The person that has been designated as the head of this process should:

- Develop plans for internal controls
- Perform control activities such as risk assessments and reviews,
- Develop and carry out a plan to correct any material weaknesses or deficiencies
- Prepare a final report

Next, guidelines for internal control reporting are to be determined. Finally, the manager of the process is to decide what employees are to be involved in the process. The employee's chosen should possess an adequate amount of knowledge regarding any evaluations and assessments that are to be performed. Their responsibilities should be clearly defined and all necessary training regarding internal controls should take place.

Segmenting the agency

Segmenting the agency is necessary dependant upon the size of the corporation. This involves dividing the corporation into separate areas to be reviewed. This is often referred to as assessable or accountable units. This segmenting makes it easier to conduct thorough evaluations and risk assessments. When segmenting the agency, management should conduct a cost-benefit analysis to determine what units are to be segmented. During this process, the personnel that are assigned to the different segments should be sufficient enough where all the necessary work will be completed in a timely fashion. For example, a multi-national corporation may have to divide the corporation into assessable units such as Finance and inventory. This may be done because the corporation is too large an entity to review as a whole. This division allows for each unit assessed separately and more efficiently. It may not be necessary to segment the agency for smaller corporations.

Common evaluation techniques

An important step in adequately assessing internal controls over financial reporting is to categorize accounts by level of significance. Once the accounts have been properly categorized an evaluation of each account should be completed in order to determine their respective levels of impact they have on the corporation and its' financial statements. Categorizing these accounts also help senior management to assess risk and develop steps that can be taken in order to off set as much risk as possible. In addition to mitigating risk, categorization may also help management define additional internal controls that may be necessary for a specific category of account as well as, more easy assess whether an existing internal control is working properly. It is also important that all personnel involved in financial reporting understand the reporting process and how information flows from one department to the next. Finally, testing of internal controls over financial reporting ensures that controls are successfully preventing errors or misstatements and/or erroneous data entry pertaining to financial statements.

Reporting process

Controls over documentation

Documentation and internal controls over documentation for financial reporting often varies by the size and the nature of business of a corporation. The appropriate personnel should verify all information contained in financial documents before making a final assessment. Guidelines should be provided in the assessment of financial documentation and plans of action to be taken regarding the assessment. It is also important for documents to be maintained and properly stored in a manner that makes the information readily available when necessary. Internal controls over accessibility to financial data and materials should also be in place in order to prevent unauthorized access. Restricting access to key personnel will help to prevent acts of collusion or fraud.

Reportable conditions

Financial reporting – Reportable conditions in financial reporting are similar to those of internal controls wherein a failure or point of weakness is found. In financial reporting though, a reportable condition involves the corporations' ability to report financial data reliably, accurately and that those reports do not conflict with laws, regulations and GAAP. A failure in internal controls in financial reporting is also considered a reportable condition when it is found not to be an isolated incident. During an investigation, if it is found that there is a good chance these failures will occur with some degree of frequency and a small probability of early detection of these failures then it considered a reportable condition. As with all reportable conditions, weaknesses should be discussed and new guidelines should be outlined and implemented to improve upon internal controls and help prevent future reportable conditions and material weaknesses.

Financial audits – A reportable condition exists when an internal control is found to be failing or has points of weakness. These failures or weaknesses in internal controls must be significant enough to be found to have a negative effect on financial reporting. Some common examples of what is considered to be a reportable condition are the following:

- Inadequate segregation of duties
- Failure to monitor activities such as business transactions, data inputs and outputs
- Controls are not adequate enough to protect assets from unnecessary loss or risk
- Abuse of authority by upper level management
- Data entry such as reconciliation is not prepared properly or in a timely manner
- Previous material weaknesses or deficiencies of internal controls have not received adequate follow-up and any material weaknesses that present the possibility of violating any laws, regulations or provisions in contracts or grants.

Criteria, condition, cause and effect as they pertain to reporting standards for financial audits:

- *Criteria:* This refers to the source of the information and the actual information the auditor uses and identifies in the audit report.
- *Condition:* The auditor should provide evidence of his or her findings during the course of the audit.
- *Cause:* The auditor should refer to the causes of any reported findings during the course of the audit. It is also imported for the auditor to state why these causes have contributed to any positive or negative findings. These findings should also be considered when making recommendations for improvements over internal controls where applicable.
- *Effect:* The auditor should state the direct effect between the conditions found and the criteria used to find those conditions.

OMB reporting objectives

The main objectives of internal control over financial reporting as presented by the OMB:

- *Existence and occurrence:* All transactions stated in reports occurred during the period dates on the reports, all assets are accounted for and all liabilities are truthfully and properly reported.

- *Completeness:* Financial reports are to include a complete list of all assets and liabilities. Management should also take care to ensure that no unauthorized transactions are included in these reports.

- *Rights and obligations:* The corporation is legally bound to all listed liabilities and all assets are legally owned at the time of reporting.

- *Valuation:* The value of all reported assets is to be reported accurately and all costs are reported as accurate and attached to the appropriate accounts.

- *Presentation and disclosure:* All financial reports are in accordance with guidelines, laws and regulations and documented in the proper format. All necessary disclosures are to be included in the financial reports.

- *Compliance:* All financial reporting must adhere to applicable laws and regulations. Finally, financial reports should confidently ascertain that adequate measures have been taken toward the protection of assets against fraud, abuse and misuse and should be made readily available for review.

Financial reporting standards

Reports regarding fraud, Illegal acts and breaches of contract and grant agreements – All relevant information regarding fraud, illegalities or breaches in contract and grant agreements should be included in the audit report. This includes any acts that have occurred or have a significant possibility of occurring. All tests or research done that has led to these findings must be identified and included in the report and should also be verified by management before coming to a conclusion. In cases where the violations are found to be insignificant, the auditor should communicate those findings to upper management of the corporation. Auditors should use professional judgment and knowledge regarding the significance and reporting of conditions that are found to be of little consequence. Even if the auditor believes that an illegal or fraudulent act has or is likely to occur, a final decision regarding legality and fraud may have to be determined by the appropriate regulatory body or court system.

Confidential or privileged information – If it is found that the auditor is bound by law to not disclose certain information, this should be noted along with the reasons why it must be excluded in the report and a general summary regarding that information should be completed. The auditor may also prepare a separate report for official use only that includes the confidential information. When making the decision to exclude confidential or privileged information from the auditor report, the auditor should consult with an attorney with adequate knowledge or specialization in order to make an accurate determination of exclusion. Finally, when deciding whether or not to exclude certain information, the auditor should consider the effect it may have on the final audit report.

The standard for financial audits regarding issuance of the audit report and its' distribution – All completed audit reports should be submitted to the appropriate officials and/or regulatory bodies in a timely manner. Reports that contain confidential or classified information, the auditor should a make a note regarding whether or not the report is intended for public or private use. Auditors conducting non-government audits should follow the guidelines and agreements described by the corporation contracting the auditor. External auditors should also note who is to receive the audit report and its' availability to the public. Internal auditors should issue reports following specific corporate guidelines. If the audit is not completed, the auditor should issue an official letter that addresses the issues of why it was not completed and the circumstances that led to its' incompletion.

The updated financial reporting standards apply both AIPCA and GAGAS standards. Auditors must report whether or not a corporation's financial statements are prepared in accordance with GAAP and report any information that does not adhere to GAAP standards. Inconsistencies between the present audits as compared with the previous audits should also be noted. Any indications of fraud, illegal use of assets, abuse or misappropriation of funds or assets are also to be reported. Finally, the auditors' opinions and conclusions should be clearly stated and understood. If the auditor has come to the conclusion that he or she does not have a concise opinion, the reasons for such a decision must be clearly stated. GAGAS standards should be applied if the auditor indicates on the report that these standards are being used. In addition to the AIPCA standards stated above, the auditor must report his or her opinions on responsible parties and include information that is considered to be restricted or confidential.

<u>Manager reporting</u>

An internal controls report must contain a statement of assurance. This statement should include findings relating to material and the course of action expected toward the correction of such weaknesses. According to the OMB, there are 3 accepted forms of statements of assurance:

- *Unqualified:* Where there are no findings of significant material weaknesses
- *Qualified:* Where there are a small number of material weaknesses to report
- *Statement of no assurance:* Where findings indicate a significant number of material weaknesses

Before statements of assurance are made a careful and thorough investigation should be conducted and findings should be closely analyzed. Management is also responsible for reporting on whether or not internal controls are successfully functioning toward the achievement of corporate goals.

<u>State and local government reporting</u>

State and local government audits are divided into two categories: Reporting Units and Opinion Units. State and local governments' Reporting Units are further divided into the following three units:

- *Primary Government-Government-wide level:* This unit covers all governmental and business activities.
- *Primary Government-Fund level:* This unit covers government and enterprise funds, internal service, agency and pension, investment and private use trust funds.
- *Component Units:* This unit covers all component units. State and local governments are required to report on all of the described units, though they are not required to give an opinion regarding all the reporting units. All Opinion Units however, must include opinions. The units in which State and Local Governments must give opinions are the following:

Governmental and business activities, all major government funds, all major enterprise funds and cumulative or aggregate funds such as internal service, agency, pension investment and private use trust funds.

Attestation engagements

The three levels of attestation engagements:

- *Examination:* Auditors must thoroughly examine all information and review results from tests conducted throughout the course of the audit before drawing complete conclusions or opinions.

- *Review:* Once comprehensive testing has been completed, the auditor must review the information that was used as a basis for the conclusion and the means by which the auditor came about the information. The auditor should also determine whether or not the information gathered conforms to the stated criteria and is presented in a fair and reasonable manner.

- *Agreed-Upon Engagements:* Auditors must conduct the audit and reporting and tests according to the agreed upon procedures specified by relevant officials.

The GAAS reporting standards for attestation engagements – Reports for attestation engagements must clearly identify the subject of the engagement:

The reports must also include the auditors' definitive conclusions and explanations as to how the auditors reached their conclusion.

The auditors should include any matters or personal impairments, which may lead them to be hesitant in regard to performing the engagement any biases or personal judgments specific to the subject of the engagement.

When making determinations regarding the availability of reports and information contained in documentation, the auditor should follow agreed upon procedures.

Finally, the report should include how and by whom it is to be used, this includes management, government bodies and oversight boards and which individuals are considered to be relevant or irrelevant parties.

The basics for general AIPCA Field Work Standards for Attestation Agreements – All fieldwork is to have proper and thorough planning and all persons involved must be provided with adequate and proper supervision. All those involved must possess the proper knowledge of internal control standards and all evaluations, tests and assessments of those standards must be clearly explained. The type of evaluations, assessments and tests to be used during the audit must also be made clear and a time frame for the expected performance of these activities should be clearly laid out. Evidence gathered throughout the course of the audit should be carefully reviewed and sufficiently support the auditor's opinions and conclusions.

The new standards also note that auditors should previous reports that contain information on deficiencies or weaknesses in internal controls as well as, review and evaluate the changes that have been made to improve upon stated weaknesses.

If the auditor specifies that he or she is using GAGAS standards in attestation reports, then the following standards are required and must be applied:

- Auditors must discuss their plans for all testing, reporting and gathering information to the appropriate corporate or federal agency officials.

- Auditors should clearly define and communicate their responsibilities to the necessary and appropriate officials.

- Auditors should take care to effectively communicate with the relevant officials or regulatory bodies along with the relevant corporate executives throughout the course of the audit. If the audit cannot be completed or is ended early, the auditor should write a letter of memorandum addressing the issues as to why and under what circumstances the audit was ended.

GAGAS Standards for Attest Documentation – All reports regarding the planning, conduction and reporting of an attestation engagement must contain enough complete information for an auditor who is not directly involved to understand the documentation. All attest documentation must also include information that substantiates all findings and conclusions before a final report is issued. Attest documentation provides the necessary information explaining how and why the auditor came to his or her conclusion as well as addressing any actual or likely instances of abuse. The attestation documentation should also contain a sufficient amount of detail in regard to its purpose, how conclusions and recommendations were reached as well as, the basis for those conclusions and recommendations.

Some additional items that should be included in attestation documentation not specifically addressed by GAGAS or AIPCA – The objectives, scope and methods used for the attestation engagement should be documented and explained. If certain standards were not followed in the engagement, the reasons for, and the effect of not following those standards should be fully explained. All activities regarding information gathered and tests performed to reach conclusions should be documented and examined. Auditors' should also explain his or her reasoning behind the overall nature of the audit, including timing and planning. If it is found that the information gathered is not sufficient enough to achieve the main goals of the engagement, the auditor must substantiate why this has occurred. All attestation documentation should be made readily available. Audit organizations should have guidelines in place that address the availability of reports by outside parties.

Independent auditor's responsibility regarding internal control

Auditors are required to determine the effectiveness of internal controls over financial reporting as part of their audit processes. This is done by testing the internal controls purported by management to look for gaps, inaccuracies, or other opportunities to change the data provided for reporting. Effective internal controls are one of the main ways an independent auditor is able to make reasonable assurances that the financial reporting is accurate and reliable.

Management vs. auditors report on internal control

After testing the internal controls, the auditor forms an opinion on the effectiveness of the internal controls and presents the results to the management team. During this presentation, the auditor must determine whether management is required to present the findings in its annual report on internal control over financial reporting. Upon completion of the presentation, the auditor is required to get written representations from management acknowledging their responsibility for establishing and maintaining effective internal controls and describing any issues that have been unearthed as a result of the audit.

Auditing

Types and objectives

External peer review procedures

Peer reviews are required for auditing agencies every 18 months if the last peer review was modified or contained negative information. These reviews will continue for every 18 months until the peer review is unmodified and free of negative information. If the overall peer review is positive and unmodified, the review period is every 3 years if the agency does not elect for a 5-year period or does not meet enhanced quality assurance standards or if the last peer review did not contain negative or modified information and the agency decides to adopt enhanced quality assurance standards. These standards include the following:

- A detailed description of the agencies quality assurance standards that must be openly available to the public
- The review of internal controls must meet specified standards
- A written statement regarding the efficiency of internal controls

Private vs. public sector auditing: Both public and private sector audits have the same basic similarities:

- Evaluating internal controls
- Reviewing financial statements in order to ensure that they are reliable and all assets and liabilities are accounted for accurately
- Making sure that all business activities adhere to all laws, rules and regulations

A major difference between public and private sector auditing is that public entities operate using public funds; therefore there is often a higher level of accountability in the public sector. Public entities must account for the uses of all public funds and resources. Public entities also have to take into careful consideration the publics' perception of the value of the service the entity is offering. Auditors and auditing committees should be comprised of well-qualified individuals whom do not have any direct activity with the day-to-day dealings of the entity. This autonomy is necessary because views can be skewed and errors of judgment or bias can occur if the individual is directly involved with day-to-day operations.

Types of auditing

Financial auditing: Financial auditing is performed in order to ensure that all financial statements are accurate and reliable and that there are no misstatements regarding assets and liabilities. These audits are also performed in order to ensure that there is no evidence of fraud and that all laws, rules and regulations are being followed. The methods used in financial reporting are quantitative and do not involve subjectivity on the auditors part. As opposed to other methods of auditing, financial auditing does not generally use a cost-benefit analysis. Financial audits are also performed in order to ensure that internal controls such as controls over accounting, cash handling, asset allocation and acquisitions are properly performing.

Contract auditing: Contract auditing is performed in order to make certain that all parties involved are fulfilling the terms of the contract. These audits are also performed to ensure that contractors and grantees are complying with all laws, rules and regulations and that the contractor receives adequate compensation for services provided. Conducting contract audits is also necessary to ensure that all awards and payments are utilized by the contractor in the manner in which the funds were intended. The information gathered in a contract audit is often used in the determination of awarding future contracts. A contract audit is also often used at the completion of the contract in order to independently review final payments, revenues and expenses of the contract.

Grant auditing: Similar to contract auditing, grant audits are conducted in order to ensure that the grantee is in compliance with all laws, rules and regulations and to ensure that the funds awarded are being utilized in the manner in which is described in the grant proposal. Grant audits are conducted to evaluate the efficiency of the grant program and whether or not it is progressing toward and meeting its' stated goals and objectives. Grant audits also provide both the grantee and federal agencies the ability to review stated goals and objectives with actual goals and objectives. If, at the conclusion of this review it is found that the systems currently in place and the activities performed are not achieving or progressing toward stated goals and objectives, contingency plans can be developed in order to better progress toward and achieve stated goals and objectives.

Compliance auditing: Compliance audits are conducted in order to ensure that federal agencies and corporations are in compliance of all applicable laws and regulations as well as, determining whether or not they are fulfilling all of their other applicable legal obligations and responsibilities. Another main purpose for compliance auditing is to ensure that adequate controls are in place in order confidently ensure that compliance is achieved and that it will continue to be achieved in the future. All non-compliance discoveries should be fully disclosed and a plan should be developed and implemented toward the goal of achieving compliance. All issues of non-compliance should be followed up by a review to determine whether the developed plan toward compliance has been successfully implemented.

Internal control auditing: The main purpose of internal control auditing is to evaluate whether adequate policies and procedures of a federal agency or corporation are in place in order to achieve stated goals and objectives. Internal control auditing helps to ensure compliance with all applicable rules, laws and regulations, to deter and prevent collusion, illegal or fraudulent activities and to ensure that all data and information regarding the federal agency or corporation is truthful, reliable and accurate. Internal control audits allow for corporate and federal agency officials to detect any material weaknesses and/or deficiencies and to develop and implement a plan of action in order to correct these weaknesses and deficiencies. These audits are also conducted in an effort to help prevent illegal activities, fraud, abuse and/or collusion.

Performance auditing objectives

Performance audits are conducted in order to provide a corporation with an unbiased and objective evaluation of operations, accountability, internal controls, program success and the compliance with applicable laws, rules and regulations. Performance audit subjects can be both narrow and broad and cover a wide variety of areas. Auditors are to discuss opinions on improvement in areas of weakness with management. These opinions are also to be included in the auditors' reports. Performance audits utilize more qualitative methods as opposed to the quantitative methods.

Performance audits analyze the use of assets, examine historical performance, involve cost-benefit analyses and evaluate the efficiency of corporation or entity as a whole.

Economy and efficiency auditing

The main objectives of economy and efficiency audits are:

- To assess whether or not the corporation or federal agency is adequately safeguarding its' assets and resources
- If it is operating in an economic and efficient manner
- If it is in compliance with applicable laws rules and regulations

If it is found that a corporation or federal agency is operating inefficiently, economy and efficiency audits are performed in order to determine the causes for this inefficiency. Economy and efficiency audits are also performed to assess procurement practices, review hiring practices in order to determine whether or not the federal agency or corporation is overstaffing and to review operating procedures in order to assess whether or not capital resources are being utilized to there full capacity.

Program effectiveness auditing

The main objectives for program effectiveness auditing in to review and determine whether the federal agency is achieving the stated goals and objectives of the program as well as, compliance with rules, laws and regulations. Program effectiveness auditing is also a tool in assessing whether or not the program remains relevant, if the program is achieving its' goals effectively and economically, to develop and review contingency plans that may help the program to achieve its' stated goals and objectives, a review of controls over management reporting and monitoring specific to the program and to identify any activities or issues that may be preventing the program from achieving stated goals and objectives.

Single audit

Corporations and non-federal agencies that spend more than $500,000 in federal grants or awards per fiscal year must conduct a single audit or program specific audit for that year. Corporations and non-federal agencies that spend less than $500,000 per fiscal year in federal grants and awards are not subject to federal audit requirements. Instead, reports regarding the appropriation of federal grants and awards must be prepared and made readily available for review by the GAO. Single audits do not include awards granted and expending through government procurement contracts regarding grants or procurement contracts for the specific purpose of purchasing goods and services. The single audit includes the audit of the non-federal agency and corporations' financial statements as well as, an audit of the federal awards granted and how those funds were appropriated.

Scope: GAGAS standards for auditing financial statements and programs must be applied when conducting *single audits.* Auditors must gain an understanding, conduct adequate testing and prepare reports regarding the non-federal agency or corporations' internal controls. The auditors must also conduct tests in order to ascertain whether the terms of the contracts or grant agreements have been or are currently being fulfilled, as well as tests to ensure that the non-federal agency or corporation is in compliance with all applicable laws, rules and regulations. The auditors must prepare reports on their findings that include the auditor's opinion of the financial statements. All previous audits should be reviewed and any significant findings from previous audits should be pursued.

Program compliance: Auditors must follow GAGAS standards regarding compliance when conducting single audits. The Single Audit Act dictates additional requirements in which the auditor must follow when conducting a single audit. These additional requirements include the following:

- The auditor must put forth what is described as a "significant effort" toward ensuring that the corporation or non-federal agency is in compliance with all applicable laws, rules and regulations. This must include ensuring that has been no violations in the provisions of federal grants, contracts and awards that have a significant effect on major programs.
- All testing conducted must include the investigation of transactions relating to the federal grants, awards and contracts. Auditors must obtain an adequate amount of evidence to support all findings.

Schedule of findings and questioned cost report:

- A written summary of audit results
- All financial statement discoveries that are considered reportable according to GAGAS
- Material weakness and/or deficiencies over internal controls that are determined to be reportable conditions, of major programs.
- Any significant, material non-compliance issues regarding contract and grant provisions and applicable rules, laws and regulations.
- Any violations of federal awards, grants and contract agreements.
- Any existing questionable costs exceeding $10,000.
- Any actual discoveries of fraudulent and/or illegal activities.
- If the auditors' opinion is not an unqualified opinion, a report explaining this opinion must be prepared.

Follow-up process: The single audit follow-up procedures dictate that auditors should review prior audit findings and conduct tests in order to assess whether the audittee has taken the appropriate measures toward the correction of any prior negative findings. If the summary schedule prepared by the audittee is found to be unreliable or the auditor has reason to believe that the audittee has misrepresented the corrective actions taken toward the curing negative findings of prior audits, then the auditor must report this as a current year finding. The auditor must conduct prescribed follow-up procedures and activities for findings that have a direct effect on major programs regardless of whether or not those findings apply to major programs in the current year being audited.

Four reports: According to the Single Audit Act, the following reports must be prepared and submitted to the applicable governing body when conducting a single audit:

- The auditors' opinion regarding whether or not the financial statements are prepared according to GAAP, reliable and fairly stated.
- The auditors' opinion of whether the federal award is adequately represented in the preparation financials statements.

- The auditor must prepare a report regarding any material deficiencies or weakness of internal controls over financial management activities.
- Any material deficiencies or weaknesses of internal controls over major programs.
- Compliance and non-compliance issues regarding the provisions of the contract or grant agreement and all applicable rules, laws and regulations.
- Any discoveries of questionable costs.

Standards

GAO independence standard

Auditors must remain unbiased and impartial throughout the course of the audit and free from all personal and organizational impairments. If an auditor does not remain unbiased, the validity of the audit and the reliability of their recommendations and opinions may come into question. Auditing agencies are required to develop and implement policies and procedures to help ensure auditor and organizational independence. The GAO point out that certain activities clearly affect an auditor and an agency's independence, such as an auditor that is an employee of agency conducting an audit for the agency in which he or she is employed. Other activities such as advising on certain matters, providing training and preparing drafts of financial statements, do no affect auditor independence.

The GAO presumes auditor agency independence in the following situations:
- If the audit agency is based out of a government agency other than the agency being audited.
- If the audit agency is based out of a different branch of government other than the branch or agency being audited.
- If the agency head is elected by a legislative body and is responsible for reporting to only that legislative body.
- When the head of an agency is appointed by a governing body outside of the governing body that is being audited.
- If the agency head is appointed or elected by someone outside any legislative body.

The GAO also presumes auditor agency independence for internal auditing when the agency is responsible for reporting to the head of a federal agency and does not hold a management or staff position in the department being audited.

Professional judgment standard

Auditors must use their professional judgment throughout the course of the audit. These professional judgments should be used to the best of the auditor's ability when planning, performing tests, gathering relevant information and data, evaluations and reporting. Auditors should not make assumptions and should utilize the concept of professional skepticism regarding the activities, products and services of the federal agency or corporation being audited. All conclusions made by the auditor should be given with supporting evidence as to how those conclusions were drawn. Another important note is that auditors, auditing agency and the corporation or federal agency being audited cannot provide absolute assurances on internal controls, business activities and errors or misstatements of financial data. It is only required that reasonable assurance regarding material deficiencies and reportable conditions be provided and obtained.

Competence standard

When auditing agency assigns auditors, the agency should make sure that all auditors:

- Possess adequate professional knowledge and competence in applicable auditing standards such as GAGAS, GAO and AICPA standards
- Obtain overall and general knowledge regarding the operations of the federal agency or corporation being audited
- Possess adequate communication skills as well as the appropriate skills to complete all audit tasks.
- Possess adequate knowledge regarding the fieldwork standards for various audits.
- Auditors conducting financial audits should be knowledgeable and familiar with GAAP.

It is important to note auditors are not required to possess all of the skills described above. The auditing agency staff of auditing agencies should possess these skills as a collective whole.

Personal impairments

The GAO classifies events that can lead to bias as personal, external and organizational. Personal biases include the following:

Anyone employed at the corporation with which the auditor has a close personal relationship. The auditor has a b, if the auditor currently or in the past has held a position where he or she had responsibility over the corporations' financial accounts.

The auditor has his or own personal judgments including political, religious, social or ideological beliefs regarding the corporation. The auditor is actively looking to be employed by the corporation at the same time the audit is being conducted.

Auditor independence

Internal controls over auditor independence include:

- Developing guidelines to help identify possible biases
- Providing proper and thorough training of auditors to help auditor's recognize possible and existing conflicts of interest
- The provision of disciplinary guidelines in cases where biases exist, but were not reported by the auditor

Audit organizations may also help to resolve personal biases with the individual auditor.

Finally, if the audit organization also provides non-audit services for a corporation, a careful evaluation of those services should be conducted in order to determine whether or not the non-audit services are creating a conflict of interest for the audit services.

GAO's yellow book

Independence rules as they apply to non-auditing activities – The GAO's updated "Yellow Book" Independence Rules as they apply to non-auditing activities address the issue of non-audit and/or consulting services and of when it may not be appropriate for auditors to perform both audit and non-audit services.

- Auditors may not perform duties in a management capacity.
- Auditors may not self police or evaluate their own work.

- Auditors should not be involved in non-audit services that have a significant or direct impact or effect on the audit.
- Auditors may accept non-audit work if the above guidelines and the following conditions are met:
- Auditors performing non-audit work are not involved with work of the audit.
- The audit services take precedence over the non-audit or consulting services.
- The level of audit activity to complete the audit accurately will not be reduced to a point where non-audit activity is the greater of the two.
- The level of audit quality and documentation requirements should also be met.
- Auditors may not be involved in certain record keeping or accounting services and may only be involved in pay roll services in a limited capacity. They may however, give clients advice regarding these activities.

Continuing Professional Education – A minimum of 80 hours of continuing professional education is to be completed every 2 years. This minimum requirement pertains to all auditors acting under the rules and guidelines Government auditing standards. This continuing education should directly apply to the improvement of increased knowledge and proficiency of the auditors work. The GAO has noted that the continuing professional education requirements as dictated by its' office may not be the same as the requirements dictated by other agencies such as state licensing boards and professional organizations. Individuals should make certain that they review the necessary requirements for such entities. It is also important to note the changes made to paragraph 46 concerning continuing professional education. Parts of this paragraph have been changed or deleted regarding continuing professional education credits. Individuals should take care when choosing the subject matter of continuing education and only subjects that pertain specifically to an individual's job should be pursued.

General auditing standards – Auditors and auditing agencies must maintain a level of autonomy in order to reach objective and impartial conclusions and recommendations. The three classes defined by the GAO Yellow book that may impair an auditor's objective judgment are personal, external and organizational.

- Personal impairments can include personal relationships or beliefs that may affect the auditors' judgment and therefore prevent the auditor from performing his or her duties objectively and impartially.
- External impairments can occur when the auditor is experiencing pressure that is actual or perceived by corporate executives and/or employees.
- Organizational impairments can occur when the auditors' judgment is affected due to the auditors' and/or the auditors' agency position within the government.

In cases of impairment auditors should excuse themselves from such projects. If this is not possible, a statement regarding the impairments should be included in the audit report.

GAGAS standards

Any pervious audit results and/or follow-up results that are of significance and have a direct bearing on the current audit should be reviewed and considered by the auditor. A careful review of previous audits and attestation engagements are important due to the fact that they could have an affect on the results of the current audit. When reviewing materials, auditor should use professional judgment and knowledge as to what is considered to be significant to the current audit. These steps should be taken in order to ensure that the work of the current auditor and past auditor is beneficial to the corporation toward the goal of efficiency and meeting stated corporate goals.

OMB Circular A-133

Circular A-133 was designed by the OMB in order to provide a uniform manner in which federal audit agencies conduct audit of non-federal agencies that receive federal awards and grants. Single audits or program specific audits must be conducted for all non-federal agencies that spend $300,000 or more in the fiscal year of federal award monies. A program specific audit may be conducted if the federal award money pertains to only one major program. Non-Federal agencies that spend less than $300,000 in federally awarded monies are considered to be exempt for these auditing requirements. The general scope of this type of audit regarding financial statements, internal controls, compliance and follow-up are relatively the same as when performing audits for entities that are not receiving government funds. Additional requirements for reporting include submitting the audit information collected, in proper form to a federal clearinghouse designated by the OMB.

FCPA guidelines

Anti-Bribery provisions – The Anti-Bribery provisions as dictated by the FCPA apply to all persons or businesses acting in the interest of a corporation. Anti-Bribery provisions state that it is unlawful to accept or offer corrupt payments or bribes to a foreign official with the purpose of gaining an unlawful advantage over competitors. Business transactions made by a U.S. corporation both inside and outside U.S. territories are subject to Anti-Bribery provisions. If these provisions are violated either within the United States and its' territories or outside the United States involving foreign countries, individuals and corporations shall be held liable and prosecuted to the fullest extent of the law. The parent companies of multi-national corporations are held responsible for activities performed by foreign subsidiaries. The following are specific provisions:

- *Corrupt Intent:* It is not necessary for the acts surrounding the illegal bribe or payment to actually take place. It is only necessary to prove that the person or business offering the alleged illegal payment has the *intention* of influencing, convincing or coercing a person's acts or decisions in order to gain an unlawful advantage over competitors or to circumvent established laws, rules and regulations.

- *Payment:* A payment is considered anything that is of value and is not restricted to currency. It is a violation of FCPA statues for persons or businesses to provide an offer or promise to pay with anything that is of monetary value in return for business favors that will lead to an unlawful advantage over competitors or to by-pass established laws, rules and regulations.

- *Business Purpose Intent:* It is a violation of anti-bribery statutes for a person or business to offer an unlawful bribe with the intention of acquiring new business or in order to retain old business. For example, corporations or corporate officials cannot offer monetary payment or any other form of payment in exchange for an award of new contracts or for the retention of old contracts. It is important to note that there are few exceptions to the anti-bribery provisions. Offering payment during the course of what is considered routine government business or activity is not considered an act of bribery and does not violate the FCPA.

- *Third Party Payments:* Third Party payments refer to the use of a go-between or intermediary in order to facilitate unlawful and illegal payments.

Permissible payments and affirmative defenses – Payments offered in the course of performing routine governmental duties such as the procurement of government documents, necessary licenses and permits, payment of utility services such as phone, water, gas and electricity and under certain circumstances, the provision of police protection are not considered unlawful. It is important to note that transactions similar to those described above are included as permissible payments and any question as to the legality of a transaction should be directed toward legal counsel to be sure that no violations are occurring. Affirmative defenses provide the person or business accused of offering an unlawful payment or promise of payment an opportunity to prove that the payment was made in the course of performing routine governmental duties. The accused or defendant is responsible for proving that the first payment was offered legally and that no FCPA statues were violated.

Sanctions against bribery:

- *Criminal Sanctions* – Corporations are subject to a fine of up to $2,000,000 and up to 5 years in prison. Individuals such as stakeholders, executives, corporate officers, employees and agents are subject to fines of up to $1,000,000 and up to 5 years in prison. If an individual is found guilty of corrupt practices, his or her fine must be paid personally and not by the employer.
- *Civil Sanctions* – Civil action may be brought against any firm or individual acting in the interests of the firm, for violations of the FCPA. These sanctions include a fine of up to $10,000. The court, SEC, Attorney General or other government agency can impose additional fines between $5,000 and $500,000.

Other actions that can be taken by the government when violations of the FCPA are discovered:

- *Other Government Actions* – Any business or persons found in violation of the FCPA can be ordered to cease and desist business activities as dictated by the Office of Management and Budgets guidelines. An indictment of a business or individual can lead to the loss of business licenses that include but are not limited to import/export licenses and securities licenses and the corporation may be banned from conducting any business with a federal government.

- *Private Cause of Action* – Competing businesses may bring additional charges pertaining to the Racketeer Influence and Corrupt Organizations Act and other laws and legislation regarding unfair business practices performed by a corporation indicted for violations of the FCPA.

FMFIA

The Federal Managers Financial Integrity Act (FMFIA) was established to amend the Accounting and Auditing act of 1950. This act was instituted for the objective of providing further assurance that corporations are complying with all applicable laws and regulations and that capital assets are reasonably protected against fraud, misappropriation and misuse. All financial data reported is to be reliable and complete and all revenue and expenses are to be included in financial reporting. The FMFIA also requires that all internal controls regarding accounting and administration are evaluated and those evaluations are to be reported. If any material weaknesses are found, those weaknesses should be included in the report as well as, plans and guidelines toward the improvement of stated weaknesses. All reports are to be made readily available to the public except in cases of national security or defense or where laws strictly prohibit public viewing. Finally, a separate report should be prepared stating that all financial reports are in compliance with GAAP and/or other standards in accounting.

1984 Single Audit Act

The Single Audit Act of 1984 states that all entities receiving government funds have adequate internal controls in place to manage the funds and the federally funded program efficiently and that the entity is compliant with all applicable laws, rules and regulations. This act was amended in 1996 (OMB circular A-133) in order to achieve consistency in audits performed regarding entities receiving federal funds. The amendment states that successful internal controls systems must be in place. This refers to the proper documentation of all transactions, reliability of financial statements and reporting, the accountability of assets and liabilities and that all transactions adhere to applicable laws, rules and regulations. The amendment also states that all transactions must also comply with the terms of the government grant contract and that all assets are reasonable protected from loss due to misuse or misappropriation.

2002 Sarbanes-Oxley Act

The Sarbanes-Oxley Act of 2002 was enacted in order to reasonably protect investors of publicly traded companies from losses due to corruption or unethical business practices by management and/or other corporate executives. The Public Company Accounting Oversight Board (PCAOB), a quasi-government agency was created as a result of Sarbanes-Oxley. In addition to the creation of the PCAOB, the act also requires the following:

Publicly held companies must fully disclose internal controls relating to financial reporting

Independent auditors must attest to such disclosures

Auditors must remain independent

The creation of audit committees for publicly held companies

Personal loans to executive officers and management is strictly prohibited

Federal sentencing guidelines were changed regarding reporting misstatements or erroneous information on financial reports

New guidelines to protect corporate whistleblowers

1978 Inspector General Act

The Inspector General Act created the Offices of the Inspector General with the purpose of supervising and conducting audits of federal agencies in order to determine the efficiency of the federal agencies operations and programs and also to detect any cases of fraud, illegal activities and abuse. The Inspector General Act also requires The Offices of the Inspector General to communicate between Congress and the federal agency being audited, regarding any material deficiencies or weakness and the recommendations to cure material weaknesses and deficiencies. Audits conducted by the Offices of the Inspector General must comply with all rules, laws and regulations dictated by the Comptroller General of the United States. The Inspector General Act also dictates that any discoveries of fraud, abuse or illegal activities be reported directly to the Attorney General in a timely manner.

Clinger-Cohen Act

The Clinger-Cohen Act is combination of the Information Technology Management and Reform Act of 1996 and the Federal Acquisition Reform Act. The Clinger-Cohen Act was designed to aid federal agencies in the acquisition and procurement and management of information technology due to federal agencies increasing dependence upon computerized systems. The main purpose and goal of the Clinger-Cohen Act are to provide federal agencies a streamlined approach to the procurement and management of information technology and its' systems. This streamlined and uniform process was determined to be necessary in order to reduce government waste of time and resources that occurred due to the purchase of information technology and systems that did not adequately perform all the activities for which it was purchased.

1990 CFO Act

The main goals of the Chief Financial Officers Act of 1990 are:

To improve upon federal agencies accounting

Financial management

Financially based internal control systems in order to help deter and prevent collusion, fraud, illegal activity, misappropriation and abuse of government resources

The CFO Act also holds federal officials accountable for the reliability and validity of financial statements and information. Federal agencies are also required to provide complete, reliable and accurate financial information in a timely manner, as requested by Congress and the Executive Branch of the government in order to fully evaluate the programs offered by federal agencies. The CFO Act also requires that all major executive offices and agencies of the government designate a Chief Financial Officer.

PCAOB

The Public Company Accounting Oversight Board (PCAOB) was founded due to the increasing prevalence of corporate corruption discovered in publicly held companies.

The PCAOB further ensures that audits are prepared independent and fair manner and the information in the audit reports are truthful, informative and reliable. The PCAOB's main task is to supervise the audits of publicly held companies in an effort to protect the interests of investors and the public. Similar to other oversight boards and committees, the PCAOB provides standards in audits and attestation engagements. These standards apply to all auditing and accounting companies that perform audits on publicly held companies and do not apply to federal and other government agencies.

AICPA accepted standards

The four generally accepted standards for financial audit reporting according to AICPA:

- The report has to state whether or not it was prepared according to generally accepted accounting principles.
- If the report does not currently follow generally accepted accounting principles, but has in the past, the circumstances for these changes must be noted and explained.
- All disclosures regarding financial statements must be true, reliable and accurate. If situations should arise where information regarding financial statements is found to be inconclusive or incomplete, the circumstances that have contributed to this situation must be thoroughly explained.
- The auditor should include a clear opinion regarding financial statements and reporting in its' entirety and if it is found that the auditor cannot come to an opinion, the auditor should clearly explain why. A statement should also be made as to how much responsibility the auditor is taking.

Field work standards

There are several common performance audit field work standards for the detection legal, contractual and grant violations. If one of the main objectives in an audit is the determination of instances of violations that are legal, contractual or pertain to grant agreements, the auditor should set guidelines regarding tests and methods during the planning phase of the audit. Any violations can be complex in nature and the auditor should streamline the audit objectives in order to come to a concise conclusion. This can be done by first determining the laws and regulations that apply to significant aspects of the corporation, contracts and grant agreements. If the auditor should determine that violations have occurred he or she may choose to seek legal counsel at that time.

During the planning phase, the auditor should conduct a thorough risk assessment that should include, but not be limited to: increased exposure risk due to fraud and internal controls over the prevention of fraud or past history regarding improper business transactions.

For audit documentation for performance audits – Audit documentation should be maintained and updated throughout the course of the audit. The information should include enough information so that an experienced auditor can easily understand any conclusions or recommendations made. The documentation is regarding as the main source of information that supports the auditors' conclusions and recommendations and should include all tests conducted, the results of those tests, main objectives, main criteria used to come to conclusions or recommendations and a description of all data gathered in the audit process. The auditing agency should also make sure that safe guards are in place to prevent the loss, misplacement and misuse of audit documents.

Institute of Internal Auditors standards

The International Institute of Internal Auditors concentrates on the professional development and continuing education standards of Internal Auditors. The standards given by the IIA involve providing guidelines for best practices of internal auditors, the continuing education and development of the individual internal auditor and clearly and effectively communicating the main purposes and goals of the internal audit to all relevant parties. The IIA standards are similar to other standards such as those of the GAO and AICPA regarding auditor independence, responsibilities, impairments and performance standards. In addition to these standards, the IIA also outlines standards of professional care regarding the overall objectives, complexity and assurances of the auditing process.

Attribute standards

The Attribute Standards of the Institute of Internal Auditors:

- *Purpose, authority and responsibility:* The overall nature of the audit should be clearly defined in the audit chartered and understood by all parties involved.
- *Independence and objectivity:* As with other standards, the auditor should do his or her best to be free from preconceived judgments, ideas or feelings about the entity or its' business

- 53 -

practices. This allows the auditor to maintain the level of objectivity necessary while performing and reporting on the audit. Any and all impairments are to be disclosed in the audit report and documentation.

- *Proficiency and due professional care:* Auditors must be knowledgeable and possess the appropriate skills to perform the audit adequately.
- *Due professional care:* The auditor should have a complete understanding of the entire scope of the audit as well as, the needs of the client and audit related costs.
- *Quality assurance and improvement program:* The Chief Internal Auditor should monitor the progress and quality of the audit by developing a Quality Assurance Improvement Program.
- *Disclosure of non-compliance:* All instances of non-compliance found should be reported to the appropriate officials.

Internal auditor performance standards

The Performance Standards of the Institute of Internal Auditors:

- *Managing the internal audit activity:* The Chief Internal Auditor must effectively manage audit activity.
- *Planning:* An appropriate plan for the audit should be completed and should determine audit activities based on level of importance.
- *Communication:* The audit plan should be successfully communicated to and approved by the appropriate corporate personnel.
- *Resource management:* The audit should carefully plan and be aware of resources utilized throughout the course of the audit.
- *Policies and procedures:* The Chief Internal Auditor should develop and communicate guidelines for the performance of audit activity.
- *Coordination:* Audit plans and procedures should be communicated and coordinated with the appropriate personnel.
- *Reporting:* The Chief Internal Auditor should report significant audit findings as necessary to senior management.

FREE Study Skills DVD Offer

Dear Customer,

Thank you for your purchase from Mometrix! We consider it an honor and privilege that you have purchased our product and want to ensure your satisfaction.

As a way of showing our appreciation and to help us better serve you, we have developed a Study Skills DVD that we would like to give you for <u>FREE</u>. **This DVD covers our "best practices" for studying for your exam, from using our study materials to preparing for the day of the test.**

All that we ask is that you email us your feedback that would describe your experience so far with our product. Good, bad or indifferent, we want to know what you think!

To get your **FREE Study Skills DVD**, email <u>freedvd@mometrix.com</u> with "FREE STUDY SKILLS DVD" in the subject line and the following information in the body of the email:

    a. The name of the product you purchased.

    b. Your product rating on a scale of 1-5, with 5 being the highest rating.

    c. Your feedback. It can be long, short, or anything in-between, just your impressions and experience so far with our product. Good feedback might include how our study material met your needs and will highlight features of the product that you found helpful.

    d. Your full name and shipping address where you would like us to send your free DVD.

If you have any questions or concerns, please don't hesitate to contact me directly.

Thanks again!

Sincerely,

Jay Willis
Vice President
<u>jay.willis@mometrix.com</u>
1-800-673-8175

Nature and work standards

The IIA Nature of Work standards regarding the Risk Management, Control, Engagement Planning and Performing the Engagement:

- *Risk management:* The audit should include a thorough evaluation of the corporations' exposure to risk regarding the reliability of important information, safeguarding assets, compliance and efficacy of operations.

- *Control:* The audit should include an evaluation of internal controls and determine whether or not the internal controls in place are on line with meeting corporate goals.

- *Engagement planning:* Planning issues to be taken into consideration should include: Audit objectives, risk factors, risk management systems, control systems and opportunities for improvement to risk management and control systems.

- Documentation should be provided regarding the understanding of all relevant parties as to the objective and scope of the audit as well as, the distribution of the audit report.

- *Performing the engagement:* Auditors should clearly identify, analyze and record all necessary information regarding the audit and audit activities. All information should be sufficient, complete and relevant.

- *Communicating the results:* All communications of audit results and findings should be complete and reliable. These reports should include the relevant recommendations and opinions of the auditor.

- *Governance:* If after a thorough evaluation, deficiencies or weaknesses in corporate governance are discovered, the auditor should make give opinions and make recommendations toward the improvement of corporate governance.

- *Resource allocation:* Auditors should clearly determine the amount of resources necessary to complete the audit and clearly communicate those amounts to corporate officials.

- Finally, all non-compliance issues should be reported accordingly. Management should then develop and implement a plan toward the resolution of non-compliance issues. The progress made toward these improvements should be monitored and reported.

Significant electronic processes

There are specific GAGAS requirements for audits that are not dependent or reliant on internal controls over information technology systems. In these cases, the auditor must thoroughly include the following statements in the audit documentation:

- The reasoning used when determining the scope of the audit.
- The extent of planned audit activities.
- If the information and data gathered during the audit is not sufficient enough to achieve its' stated goals and objective, the auditor must report the effect this will have on the audit.
- The reliability of information and data gathered outside the computerized or electronic systems.

These additional requirements are necessary because if the auditor gathers information and data from a computerized system and the internal controls over that system have not been tested, the reliability and accuracy of that information comes into question.

Responsibilities

Reportable deficiencies

The following breakdowns in internal controls should be observed, investigated and reported by the auditor:

- If it is found that there is a lack of separation of duties that directly causes a breakdown in internal controls, increases risk and jeopardizes corporate goals.
- If there is not a consistent control in place to review business and accounting transactions in order to detect and prevent fraud and misstatements.
- If guidelines in place do not provide adequate assurance that all capital assets are protected or if no such guidelines exist.
- If there is found to be evidence that capital assets have been lost, misused or misappropriated due to internal control failures.
- If it is found that corporate executives or management have circumvented internal controls causing or potentially causing a breakdown in corporate objectives.
- If the auditor discovers any cases of fraudulent activity.

- If necessary steps have not been taken to improve or correct any previously reported breakdowns of internal controls.
- If necessary steps have not been taken to create a needed internal control if it had been recommended in the previous report.

Sources of information

Some common sources of information to help management assess and monitor internal controls include the following:

- Information and knowledge obtained through daily activities and operations
- Management reviews
- Reviews conducted specifically for evaluating internal controls
- Review conducted that are not specifically done so for the evaluation of internal controls, but contain internal control evaluation components
- Various reports including Inspector General and GAO reports
- Prior reports and evaluations prepared in accordance with The CFO Act, FFMIA, FISMA and OMB Circulars A-130 and A-127
- Prior annual performance plans and reports
- Previous audits
- Reviews and reports prepared in accordance with IPIA
- Prior audit, review and report results

Detection of fraud

There are basic GAGAS field work standards regarding the detection of fraud and violations of contracts, grant agreements and applicable laws. During the planning stage of the audit, the auditor should outline clear guidelines and actions planned to detect any cases of fraudulent or abusive activities. Auditors' should be aware of any information or actions that may indicate fraud, illegal activities, potential breaches of contracts and grant agreements and acts of abuse and the effect these actions have on the audit results. There are no laws or regulations that can be referred to in cases of abuse. The auditor must examine the information received and use professional judgment as to how the abuse will affect the outcome of the audit if it is found to have actually occurred.

Given the subjective nature of what is considered to be abusive, auditors are not required to provide any assurance regarding the detection of abuse. In cases of actual acts of fraud, the auditor must not interfere with investigations by regulatory bodies and/or law enforcement.

Auditee responsibilities

The auditee must effectively communicate and discuss all audit issues with the auditor and the auditing board or committee. Management of corporations and officials of federal agencies must provide full disclosures of all documentation requested by the auditor that is necessary and relevant to the conduct of the audit. Management and officials are required to report any cases of fraud or illegal activities as determined by applicable laws and regulations. They must also take the necessary steps in order to correct and cure any instances of fraud, illegal activities and abuse as recommended by the auditor and/or auditing board or committee. Auditees must also submit written requests such as Management Assertation Letters in a timely manner.

Phases

Chief Internal Auditors

The Chief Internal Auditor is an individual who is appointed by the executive management to participate in and oversee the auditing process. The roles and responsibilities of the Chief Internal Auditor are to perform and internal investigation of internal controls, compliance with applicable laws and regulations and instances of possible non-compliance with laws and regulations. The CIA is also responsible for investigating possibilities of fraud, collusion and misuse or misappropriations of corporate capital assets. Once the investigation is complete, the CIA makes recommendations to executive management and/or the audit committee, regarding improvements or changes that should be made in cases of internal control weaknesses, in order to better achieve corporate goals.

Planning process

The first stage of an audit is planning. During this stage, auditors meet with corporate executives to discuss the audit in terms of areas it plans to cover, examination and investigative processes the auditor plans to use and the major goals of the audit. At this time, management may address issues of concern to the auditor as well as resources that can be made available in order to complete the audit.

The next stage is the act of conducting the audit itself. This is when the auditor gathers relevant information through investigation. These investigation processes can include interviewing employees and reviewing relevant data files. Auditors may also observe employees when investigating the efficiency of internal controls.

At the end of the planning phase, the auditor prepares an audit program, which serves as a guideline of the necessary actions needed in order to complete the audit thoroughly and to achieve audit goals.

Performance audit planning phase

The first step toward a successful performance audit is making sure that all stages of the audit are comprehensively planned. When developing a plan, the auditor should make sure that the goals and objectives of the audit are clearly stated as well as defining the scope and methods the auditor intends to utilize in order to complete the audit. Auditors should also keep the plan flexible enough to adjust for changes as situations dictate. When planning the audit, the following should be considered:

Who will be using the audit report

What methods of testing and examination will be used throughout the audit

How well the auditor understands the subject matter or program that is to be audited

How previous audit results will be considered

The number of staff needed to successfully complete the audit

How the information will be communicated to the appropriate officials

Conducting an audit

After the planning phase has ended, the conduction phase begins. This is when the auditor will perform the fieldwork necessary in order to gather relevant information. At this time, the auditor may conduct in-depth interviews, comprehensively review internal controls and apply various testing methods that are both statistical and non-statistical. Throughout the auditing process, the auditor should communicate with management regarding any noteworthy negative discoveries. This gives management the opportunity to discuss methods to correct any problems. At the completion of the fieldwork, an audit report draft is prepared. It is then reviewed and discussed by the audit committee. After the audit committee reviews the draft, a meeting with management is conducted in order for the auditors and management to discuss the findings of the audit and to review the information contained in the audit draft. After this meeting, a final draft is prepared and the audit committee or manager reviews any changes made. If the draft does not require additional editing, a final report is prepared.

Entrance conference

The Entrance Conference is necessary for the auditor to communicate the audit plan to officials at the federal agency or corporation being audited. The auditors should discuss matters of what the audit will entail included the scope of the audit, methods to be used in gathering information and the timeframe in which the audit is expected to be completed. The Entrance Conference also allows for the auditee to discuss any issues relevant to the audit such as possible instances of fraud, collusion or abuse. While communicating the audit plan, the auditors should inform the auditee that the plan is subject to change if relevant information during arises necessitating these changes. The auditors should also provide a plan as to how they are going to keep the auditee informed of discoveries made during the course of the audit and fieldwork results.

Identifying measurement criteria

Identifying measurement criteria for performance audits is not as easy as those of financial audits. For financial audits, audit findings are measured against what is often very straightforward and objective information. Identifying measurements for performance audits is more complex due to the fact that the measurements are not as straightforward and the basis for identifying some measurement criteria may be more subjective in nature. When establishing measurement criteria, the following considerations should be made:

The stated goals of the federal agency or corporation as dictated by laws and regulations.

The federal agency or corporations stated policies and procedures.

Previously measured performance information.

Measured and reported performance of the federal agency or corporations' peers.

Best practices of the federal agency or corporations' peers.

Conducting performance audits

There are several common internal control considerations when conducting performance audits. Changes in legislative and regulatory bodies as well as changes in laws and regulations make the need for effective internal controls of the utmost importance. Auditors should take care to review the efficacy of internal controls to ensure that they are relevant to achieving stated program objectives. During the assessment of internal controls, auditors should make reasonably sure that all information gathered is reliable. It is also important the auditor review the programs complicity with applicable laws and regulations as well as review contracts and grants agreements to ensure that no violations of the provisions of these contracts or agreements have occurred. Having a full understanding of internal controls will help the auditor determine successes and failures of the program and make recommendations for improving internal controls in order to help the program toward achieving stated goals.

Analytical tests during auditing

It is necessary to conduct analytical tests throughout the course of the audit in order to obtain an overall assessment of the federal agency or corporation.

- Conducting analytical tests helps to provide substantiating evidence supporting audit findings and management assertations.
- These tests also allow the auditor to further investigate and draw conclusions upon and actual or perceived instances of fraud, abuse, misstatements and discrepancies in financial transactions and/or statements and other resource capital.
- Analytical test are also important in ensuring that all relevant information and data gathered for auditing purposes is accurate and reliable.
- These tests also provide a basis for auditor to draw comprehensive conclusions and recommendations.

Evidence

Tests of evidence: All information and data gathered for performance audits should be tested in order to determine it has any bearing on the performance of a federal agency or corporation. The evidence should meet the following criteria before being considered or identified as a measurement to be used in the performance audit:

Sufficient: The quantity of information and data gathered should be adequate enough to support any opinions or findings of the auditor.

Competent: Auditors should make sure that all the information and data gathered is accurate and reliable. Auditors should also take the necessary steps to ensure that the information and data gathered is authentic and not a product of fraudulent activity.

Relevant: All information and data gathered should be relevant to the performance audit and its' stated goals and objectives.

Audit evidence categories: The four main categories of Audit Evidence in fieldwork standards of Performance Audits:

Physical Evidence: All information and data that has been gathered through physical inspection or observation by the auditor.

Documentary Evidence: All information and data that was created. Documentary evidence often includes such items as accounting records, receipts and invoices.

Testimonial Evidence: All information and data that has been gathered by question and answer through activities such as interviews and written questionnaires.

Analytical evidence: All information and data gathered that has been analyzed through activities such as computations and/or comparisons. Analytical information should also be separated into relevant categories.

All information gathered should be thoroughly tested to ensure conformity with the GAGAS standards of sufficiency, competency and relevancy. Any evidence that does not meet these standards should be disregarded.

Exit conference

The exit conference should take place when all necessary audit fieldwork has been completed. The exit conference is a meeting between the auditor and auditee to discuss the findings of the audit and for the auditor to discuss his or her conclusions and recommendations based on these findings. The auditor then provides the auditee of a draft of the report in preparation for the final audit report.

Reporting phase

The reporting phase of the audit begins when all necessary tests have concluded and all information is gathered in order to prepare the necessary audit reports. At this time, auditors should draw their conclusions, recommendations and opinions to be included in the audit report. All audit findings should be prepared for inclusion in the final audit report at this time. The auditor may also discuss these findings with relevant federal agency and corporate officials so they can prepare their statements necessary for inclusion in the final audit report. Auditors may be required to retain all audit working papers for a prescribed period of time depending upon the type of audit that was conducted. The accessibility to these working papers should also be discussed with regulator boards as well as relevant corporate and federal agency officials.

When the audit draft report is presented to the auditee, it generally includes requests from the auditor to the auditee regarding agreement on the following subjects:

- The stated facts of the audit
- The auditor's recommendations and conclusions
- Whether or not the auditee plans to take action regarding the auditor's recommendations and conclusions.

Report quality elements: The main report quality elements of Performance audits conducted using GAGAS standards:

Timely: The auditor should be sure to report any relevant information in a timely manner while keeping the needs of the audit report users in mind. Depending on the complexity of the audit, this may include giving updates regarding as to the audits progress as well as, informing the appropriate personnel of any significant findings. These updates can be written or verbal.

Complete: The report should be complete and adequately provide information regarding audit objectives. The auditor should include all evidence that supports findings and recommendations.

Accurate: All information in the report should be reliable and accurate. The auditor should take care that all evidence is corroborated when necessary and that there are no misstatements or mistakes on the report.

Objective: The content of the report should reflect objectivity and that the auditor has maintained independence throughout the audit.

Convincing: All information presented should adequately support and validate all findings, conclusions and recommendations.

Concise: When preparing the report, the auditor should remain on point and only include necessary detail.

Reporting standards regarding form and report content for performance audits:

All audit reports should clearly communicate the results of the audit and be presented in a form that fits the needs of its users.

Reports should also be made available to the public when dictated and contain plans of action for audit follow-up regarding improvements on deficiencies discovered during the audit.

All reports must contain the goals and objectives of the audit and what actions and tests were performed in order to come to conclusions.

The contents of the report should also include statements of compliance with auditing standards and an explanation of any privileged information that may have been omitted from the audit report. The opinions and view of relevant personnel should also be included in the contents of the audit report.

Reporting standards regarding object, scope, methodology and findings of performance audits – In order for the users of the audit report to fully comprehend the findings, all objectives should be clearly stated. This avoids any potential misunderstandings by the intended users of the audit report. The auditor should also be specific when stating the extent of the work that is to be completed as well as what actions were taken regarding gathering information and tests conducted.

It is also important for the auditor to describe any limitations based on inaccessibility reliable information or necessary personnel. All findings of the audit must have supporting evidence of those findings. When reporting findings, the auditor should include the criteria, condition, cause and effect of those findings.

Regarding internal control deficiencies pertaining to performance audits – All substantial material deficiencies of internal controls found during the course of the audit should be noted on the audit report and a separate report should be prepared the corporate executives of the corporation being audited. If illegal or fraudulent acts are found to have occurred during the course of the audit, the auditor includes pertinent information regarding these acts in the audit report. Audit report information regarding fraud or illegal activities should include evidence that supports the auditors' findings, methods used and tests conducted for gathering supporting evidence. All of the relevant information should be prepared in a separate report to be provided to the appropriate officials.

Reporting standards regarding fraud, illegal activities and violations of contracts or grant agreements – GAGAS has specific reporting requirements when fraud, illegal activities and violations of contracts or grant agreements have been discovered. If an internal auditor conducts the audit, then the findings do not have to be reported to an outside party unless the auditor is bound by law. If the corporation receives funds from governmental sources, the auditor must also report the fraud to the government agency in which the corporation receives funds. Once the fraud or illegal activities have been reported to the corporate officials, those officials must then take the appropriate steps to rectify the situation. Auditors should take care in reporting negative information that is readily available for public viewing to ensure that the information does not impede any potential or ongoing investigations

Reporting standards regarding the issuing and distributing audit reports – Auditors should make sure that all necessary officials, corporate executives and regulatory and/or legislative bodies receive the audit report in a timely fashion. If audit reports contain privileged or classified information, the auditor should distribute the report only to specified designated users. Internal auditors should follow the stated corporate guidelines regarding audit report distribution. All restrictions or issues regarding the distribution and issuance of the audit report such as its' accessibility to the general public, should be stated in the audit documentation. In the case of a non-government auditor reporting under GAGAS standards, the parties whom the audit report is to be issued and distributed should be clearly stated in the engagement agreement.

Regarding laws and contract and grant agreements – If the audit conducted is done so according to GAGAS standards, whether required or by choice, the auditor must specifically state this fact in the report. Additional GAGAS standards include providing a full depiction and explanation of the tests conducted on internal controls over financial reporting and the subsequent results. Tests should include information regarding the corporations' compliance with applicable laws, contracts or grant agreements. If those tests and results are contained in a separate report, then it must be noted in the main audit report. Auditors must also assess how effective the tests conducted are in supporting the auditors' opinion or statement regarding internal controls over financial reporting as they relate to applicable laws and contract and grant agreements.

Regarding internal controls over financial reporting – Reports on internal controls over financial reporting must contain an Assurance Statement separate than that of the Assurance Statement regarding the effectiveness of internal controls. Assurance statements should describe with reasonable confidence that all financial reporting is trustworthy, adheres to guidelines, laws and regulations and that mistakes will be detected and corrected in a timely manner. Reports regarding internal controls over financial reporting also serve the purpose of making sure that corporate assets are properly utilized and there are no cases of significant loss or inappropriate use of those assets. All financial statements and business transactions should be included on financial reporting if those actions have a significant impact on corporate finances such as earnings, budgets and capital expenditures.

<u>Management representation letter</u>

The AIPCA standards for management representation letters pertaining to financial statement audits are prepared by management or officials of a federal agency or corporation and are designed to address such issues as:

- Management responsibility regarding their accountability over financial statements
- Accountability over the preparation of financial statements
- Responsibility over internal controls, legal compliance
- Auditor access to all relevant financial data
- Contingent liabilities
- Any perceived or actual cases of collusion among employees and management, or the lack thereof and any cases of illegal activities or fraud, or the lack thereof.

The legal department or counsel of the federal agency or corporation should provide to the auditor a similar letter regarding any pending and actual litigation, claims and other relevant legal issues.

Contracting an audit

When contracting for audit services, corporations and federal agencies should follow the procurement process guidelines for contracting goods and services. The federal agency or corporation should conduct a thorough investigation into the prospective auditing agencies in order to ensure that the audit to be contracted will be competently conducted according to GAO Yellow Book and GAGAS standards. The federal agency or corporation should also obtain the auditing agency's most current copy of its peer review report. When selecting an auditing agency, the federal agency or corporation should take many factors into consideration outside of price. Issues such as overall competence, independence, objectivity and professionalism of the auditing agency should also be included in deciding factors along with costs.

Audit follow-up

An audit follow-up is conducted after a stated period of time in order to determine if a plan of action is in place toward correcting material deficiencies of internal controls and all other negative findings. If management disagreed with any findings or recommendations at the time the final audit report was prepared, the matters are discussed and an attempt at resolution is made during the audit follow-up period. If the disagreements made by management at the time the final audit report was prepared pertain to laws, rules or regulations, management must find legal ground for their disagreements and prepare a written document regarding those findings. A follow-up report is then made at the conclusion of this period.

Corrective actions follow-up:
The standards of follow-up systems regarding corrective actions as dictated by the OMB:
- An audit manager must be designated to oversee the follow-up process.
- All negative findings must have a corrective action plan and begin as soon as possible.
- All plans should be in writing.
- All plans should be periodically assessed in order to evaluate progression toward corrective action and to make changes to the corrective action plan when necessary.
- Accurate documentation must be provided.
- Adequate resources are to be provided in order to ensure the plans' success and to resolve any disagreements.
- All plans are to abide by all laws and regulations.
- If there are multiple agencies involved, those agencies must be efficiently coordinated.

Resolution plans follow-up:
The standards of follow-up systems regarding resolution plans as dictated by the OMB:
- All negative findings must have a resolution plans and begin as soon as possible. OMB guidelines state that negative findings are to be cured within six months from the date of the final report or, if a non-Federal auditor completed the audit, six months from the date the applicable government office receives the report.
- Progress reports and updates on unresolved audit issues are to be given every six months to the appropriate agency head.
- Plans should be reviewed and updated as necessary.

- Performance appraisals of applicable officials should be conducted in order to ensure that the resolution plans are being implemented effectively.
- The audit follow-up system should be evaluated every year to ensure the continued success of the resolution plan.

General

Quality control and assurance

Auditing agency must develop, communicate and implement adequate internal controls regarding the monitoring of the agencies activities, policies and procedures. Periodic monitoring should be conducted in order to ensure that all auditors are adhering to the stated policies and procedures of the auditing agency. External peer review of agencies that conform to GAGAS standards must be conducted every 3 years. This is done to provide the agency with unbiased recommendations regarding material deficiencies and weaknesses in internal controls and suggestions as to how to improve upon these deficiencies and weaknesses. Auditing agencies that conform to GAGAS standards must provide a copy of the peer review report to its' respective oversight board or committee and recommends that peer reviews on government agency be made publicly available.

Program understanding

Understanding the overall program and its' significance will help the auditor to better determine the overall goals and objectives of the audit. It also aids in determining whether information or events are of significance. Auditors must fully comprehend the laws and regulations that specifically pertain to a particular program in order to correctly determine whether or not fraudulent or illegal activity exists. Fully understanding a program and its' main goal and purpose will help the auditor complete an audit report that addresses the important issues of whether or not the program is achieving or moving toward the achievement of its' stated goals, making the audit report more useful to the auditee.

Reasonable assurance

Reasonable Assurance can be described as a corporation providing reasonable assertions that unnecessary risks are not being taken and risks are reduced where possible, careful cost/benefit analyses that include all relevant non-financial costs, are performed in order to ensure that costs do not outweigh benefits, all assets are utilized efficiently and appropriately. Reasonable assurance also provides that corporations are adhering to all applicable laws, rules and regulations and that all reporting in accurate and reliable. Reasonable assurances are in place in order to hold corporations accountable for the use of corporate assets toward the achievement of stated goals. It is important to note that while reasonable assurances provide a level of confidence in the achievement of corporate goals, they cannot provide absolute guarantees that those goals will be met.

Statements of assurance

When management has finished its' assessment regarding internal controls over financial reporting they are required to come to a specific conclusion that is to be include in the Assurance Statement which must be either qualified, unqualified or no statements of assurance.

- *Unqualified Statements of Assurance* are made when there are no material weaknesses or deficiencies found in the assessment.
- *Qualified Statements of Assurance* are made when one or more material weaknesses or deficiencies are found.
- *Statements of no assurance* are made when internal controls are found not to exist or there are prevalent material weaknesses and deficiencies. If one or more material weaknesses exist, management cannot state in the statement of assurance that the internal controls over financial management are effective and adequate.

- 70 -

Assurance statements regarding internal controls over financial reporting – The Assurance statements made by management should be a comprehensive assessment of the efficiency and relevance of internal controls over financial reporting for the corporation. The requirements that must be included in assurance statements:

- Management must state what their specific responsibilities are in developing and maintaining internal controls over financial reporting
- A statement referring to OMB Circular A-123 as being used as a basis when assessing internal controls over financial reporting
- The assessment must include a specific conclusion regarding the efficacy of internal controls over financial reporting
- A statement of material weaknesses must be included as well as resolution plans to weaknesses. If weaknesses found are quickly resolved, how they were resolved should also be included in the assurance statement.

Audit costs

The following considerations should be made in order to determine allowable audit costs:

- The costs must be necessary in order to adequately perform the audit and achieve audit objectives.
- The costs must be reasonable.
- The costs must be in compliance with applicable laws and regulations.
- The costs for the same activities are purposes must be consistent.
- The costs must be in accordance with GAAP.

The following considerations should be made in order to determine non-allowable costs:

- After review of the costs, they are found to be unnecessary in order to adequately perform the audit and achieve its' stated goals and objectives.
- The costs are unreasonable.
- The costs are non-compliant with applicable laws and regulations.
- The costs cannot be allocated to a specific audit related activity.

Audit risk

Audit risk encompasses inherent risk, control risk and detection risk. Audit risk is evaluated when determining the extent at which analytical tests will be performed. The auditor must decide which material deficiencies and misstatements are significant and then determine with some degree of certainty, whether or not they are likely to occur again. If the auditor determines that the material deficiencies and misstatements have a high chance of occurring more than once, then auditor should increase the level of analytical tests to be performed. If the auditor finds that a material deficiency or misstatement is not a product of weak internal controls and is an isolated incident unlikely to occur more than once, then the auditor may decide to decrease the amount of analytical testing to be performed.

Control risk

Control risk is the risk that involves the possibility that material deficiencies and misstatements will not be discovered by internal controls. Control risk should be thoroughly evaluated in order to determine whether the internal controls in place are sufficient enough to prevent cases of fraud, abuse, illegal activities, collusion and misstatements or significant errors in financial data and reporting. If, after examination, it is found that the control risk of a federal agency or corporation is high, then plans to help mitigate these risks should be developed and implemented. Once implemented, periodic and ongoing monitoring should take place to ensure that control risk has been effectively reduced by the plan. Control risk is directly related to the efficacy of the overall internal control environment.

Inherent risk

Inherent audit risk is measured by determining the likelihood and frequency of significant errors or misstatements occurring. Although it cannot be said that mistakes will never be made, the level of acceptable risk and unacceptable risk must be determined in order for the auditor to draw comprehensive conclusions of inherent audit risk. It is important for auditors to keep in mind that some activities innately carry higher levels of inherent risk. Such activities may include cash handling and large or complex processes that, due to their nature, provide the opportunity for a greater amount of mistakes and errors. Inherent audit risk applies to both financial and non-financial processes and activities.

Detection risk

Detection risk is measured by determining the level of possibility that the auditor will not discover material deficiencies, material weaknesses, misstatements and errors. Detection risk directly correlates with the efficacy of the auditing procedures and how well the auditor carries out those stated procedures. Unlike inherent and control risks, detection risk is considered to be the only audit risk measure that is within the auditors' control. Auditors' can mitigate detection risk through the adequate planning of the audit, sufficient supervision of audit employee's, periodic reviews of audit tests, information gathered and audit documentation and increasing the frequency and/or extent in which audit tests are to be performed. All tests regarding detection risk should be relevant to achieving the audits stated objectives.

High- and low-risk criteria

In order to efficiently evaluate Federal Program risk, the auditor must evaluate the overall internal control environment in order to determine material weaknesses and deficiencies of internal controls over the federal program. The risk assessment of federal programs is necessary in order to ascertain whether the program is effective, efficient and in compliance with all applicable laws rules and regulations. The overall risk assessment may affect the amount of the federal award for the following fiscal year dependent upon whether risks are determined to be low or high.

The following are indications of high risk:
- The existence of multiple internal control structures.
- Insufficient and/or ineffective monitoring of sub-recipients.
- New or recently modified information technology systems.
- Negative findings in previous audits conducted.
- Federal programs that were not previously classified as major programs but are being audited as a newly classified as a major federal program.

The criteria that must be met for a non-federal agencies receiving federal awards and funding to be considered low risk when assessing Federal Program Risk as dictated in OMB Circular A-123, the following criteria must be met for 2 consecutive years:

- Single Audits were conducted annually.
- All auditor statements were unqualified
- No material weaknesses or deficiencies of internal controls were discovered.
- The absence of any non-compliance issues.
- No cases of questioned costs existed.

In some cases the auditor may discover material weaknesses, but the audited entity may still be considered to be low risk if the weaknesses and deficiencies discovered are found to not have an affect on the management of the federal award or grant. In such cases, a waiver must be obtained.

In order to efficiently evaluate Federal Program risk, the auditor must evaluate the overall internal control environment in order to determine material weaknesses and deficiencies of internal controls over the federal program. The risk assessment of federal programs is necessary in order to ascertain whether the program is effective, efficient and in compliance with all applicable laws rules and regulations. The overall risk assessment may affect the amount of the federal award for the following fiscal year dependent upon whether risks are determined to be low or high.

The following are indications of high risk:

- The existence of multiple internal control structures.
- Insufficient and/or ineffective monitoring of sub-recipients.
- New or recently modified information technology systems.
- Negative findings in previous audits conducted.
- Federal programs that were not previously classified as major programs but are being audited as a newly classified as a major federal program.

The criteria that must be met for a non-federal agencies receiving federal awards and funding to be considered low risk when assessing Federal Program Risk as dictated in OMB Circular A-123, the following criteria must be met for 2 consecutive years:

- Single Audits were conducted annually.

- All auditor statements were unqualified

- No material weaknesses or deficiencies of internal controls were discovered.

- The absence of any non-compliance issues.

- No cases of questioned costs existed.

In some cases the auditor may discover material weaknesses, but the audited entity may still be considered to be low risk if the weaknesses and deficiencies discovered are found to not have an affect on the management of the federal award or grant. In such cases, a waiver must be obtained.

Financial and Managerial Concepts, Controls and Techniques

Cash Management

Establishing banking relationships

When establishing banking relationships it is important to evaluate the full range of services the financial institution offers. It is also important to receive bids from various banks in order to compare them to one another. The main areas of considerations are the following:

- *Collection services:* How much time it takes to collect and deposit payments for accounts receivable and record the information connected to the deposit.
- *Concentration services:* The ease and time it takes to deposit payments from various accounts into one centralized account.
- *Investment services:* The type of services offered for earning interest on income that is not marked for immediate use.
- *Short term borrowing services:* Types of short-term credit programs offered.
- *Information reporting:* Accessibility of to account balances and transactions in order for account manager evaluation.
- *Compensating balance fund:* This refers to an account maintained by the depositor in order to adequately cover all funds borrowed.

Making timely payments

The most common form of payment is through paper checks and warrants. Checks are drawn off a bank and warrants are drawn off the treasury. If a bank specifically designated as a depository, then funds have been deposited to this account by the treasury for the purpose of paying any warrants issued. However, if the bank is not the designated depository, the bank must then pay the warrant and wait for reimbursement by the treasury. Another common technique is through the use of electronic payments. Electronic payments are offered to reduce time and resources spent on processing paper payments. EFT and ACH payments also reduce the risks of lost or stolen paper checks. Setting up an Auto Debit/Credit and recurring electronic payment accounts also reduce the time and resources spent on processing payments and help to ensure that payments are made on time. Electronic Data Interchange systems submit both payment and remittance electronically and simultaneously. Finally, the use of bankcards and stored limit cards increases efficiency in the collection of payments.

Accelerating collection

One of the first ways for accelerating collections is implementing strategies and activities to improve the ease and convenience of payments. Such activities can include night deposit boxes and offering services such as Automatic Debit, Electronic Funds Transfers or offering the ability to pay for services via the Internet and telephone. Offering electronic services often lessen the risk of the possibility of a check being returned for non-sufficient funds. Offering incentives or rewards for on time payments and penalties for late payments are also effective tools for accelerating collections. Management should also make sure that invoices are completed properly and all terms of the agreement are stated completely. It is also important that invoices are sent out in a timely manner.

- *Lockbox services*: Post office boxes maintained a financial institution where   receipts are directly mailed. Lockbox services are used as a means for accelerating collections.
- *Concentration systems:* Speeds up the process in which deposits from multiple accounts are consolidated into one centralized account. Concentration systems are used to better manage credits and debits to the account as well as offer funds that are not marked for immediate use to be transferred to investment accounts for the purpose of earning interest.
- *Web-based collections:* Offer electronic methods for collections such as ACH, EFT and credit card payments. Web-based collections offer ease of payment for the debtor and collection by the creditor.

Electronic cash management techniques

Advances made in electronics and information technology offer increased convenience for both the consumer and the corporation. The use of debit cards, electronic funds transfers, ACH and payment services offered via telephone and internet provide the corporation with immediate funds and remove delays in receiving payments associated with traditional paper-checks. In circumstances where paper checks are utilized, corporations may now use electronic check presentment. This is a process where the check image is substituted for the actual check. As with other electronic services, this decreases the risk of non-payment due to insufficient funds. Advances in software allow for financial managers to streamline inputs, outputs and other financial data. There is also a lower risk of misstatements or human error on financial statements.

Cast management legislation

Federal Legislation regarding cash management and controls over cash.

- *The Prompt Payment Act of 1982* and as amended in 1988, dictate that federal agencies must make all payments on time, and pay all penalties when payments are made late and take discounts only if they are proven to be cost effective and payments are made on or prior to the prescribed discount date.
- *The Deficit Reduction Act of 1984* dictates that all federal agencies are responsible for adequate collection and deposit practices. Whenever possible, federal agencies must utilize EFT's, Lockboxes and/or automatic withdrawal processes.
- *The Debt Collection Improvement Act of 1996* dictates that federal agencies disburse payments through electronic methods when possible.
- *The Cash Management Improvement Act of 1990* dictates that federal agencies make improvements regarding the transfer of funds between state local and federal governments.

Controls over cash

Cash presents a large set of problems if adequate controls over cash are not implemented and monitored. Of all capital resources, cash is the most susceptible to theft, misappropriation and loss through negligence. Common controls over cash include designated authorized users to make cash deposits and withdrawals as well as a means in which those deposits and withdrawals are verified and reconciled. The duties of collection, recording, deposits and reconciliation, of payments and deposits should be separated among different personnel whenever possible, in order to deter theft and collusion. Automated accounting systems should also be used whenever possible to avoid theft, collusion and material misstatements of financial records. Any perceived or actual fraudulent activities should be addressed and dealt with in an appropriate and timely fashion.

Investment management

Risk is inherent with all investments. Effective investment management involves establishing the level of acceptable risk while maintaining the financial needs and growth of the corporation. Risk factors should be measured against estimated returns for effective investment management. It is also important to determine the level of ease or difficulty in converting the investment to cash; this is often described as liquidity. Guidelines regarding the level of acceptable risk and long and short-term corporate financial goals regarding investments should be provided to investment managers and all other parties involved in investment making decisions through investment policies and procedures manuals. These manuals should dictate levels of acceptable risk versus return, the decision-making processes, requirements for investment transactions and overall investment objectives as they pertain to corporate goals.

Selecting money managers

When selecting money managers it is important to choose an individual that has sufficient knowledge of investments and understands all corporate goals and constraints regarding the investment of funds as they pertain to the corporation. Corporate executive should also be sure that the selected individual is aware of all laws and regulations regarding the act of investing as well as, all laws and regulations regarding the reporting of investments made. Executives should choose money managers whom are found to have a high level of integrity and a strong work ethic. A strong work ethic is important to ensure that the individual will investigate all investment decisions with due diligence in order to have the most complete information before making important investment decisions.

Evaluating money managers

Periodic evaluations and observations must be completed in order to assess a money manager' performance. Periodic evaluations may include examining investments made and if those investments are in line with corporate goals and auditing investment files and portfolios to be sure that all laws and regulations are being followed. The evaluation of investments decisions made by money managers allows for corporate executives to determine whether or not stated goals are to be achieved.

Periodic evaluation also helps to ensure that there are no instances of fraud, unethical behavior or that the money manager is making investment decisions involving unacceptable risk to principal. Another useful tool when evaluating a money managers' performance is benchmarking. Benchmarking is done by comparing the corporations' investments to that of industry leaders.

Managing capital investments

A financial manager must have analytical tools in order to properly invest capital. Without these tools, the financial manager does not have an adequate amount of data to make an informed decision. The following are common considerations for financial managers when making capital investment decisions:

- The dollar amount of capital needed for the investment.
- The dollar amount of funding that is available for the investment.
- The expected gains or returns from the investment.
- Legalities and government rules and regulations of making the investment.

Another important consideration for financial managers to make is measuring the opportunity cost of the investment, this is done by evaluating what projects, programs and other investments must be foregone in order to make a particular investment. Financial managers must decide whether or not the benefits from the investment outweigh the all applicable costs, including opportunity costs.

Governments and federal agencies

Governments and federal agencies are charged with the protection of public funds and to make investment decisions that are in the best interest of the general public. Governments and federal agencies focus on having the least amount of idle cash on hand as necessary. Having large quantities of cash on hand can increased theft or fraudulent activity. The government or federal agency's focus for idle cash should be on investing the amounts not needed for operating purposes. The investments made by governments and federal agencies should be relative liquid in order to easily access the cash when needed. Investments made by governments and federal agencies are generally short-term, low-risk investments, though long term investments are also made in order to meet future payment obligations such as those to pension and endowment funds.

Risks defined

All investments involve a certain level of risk due to the uncertainty of a guaranteed return. Investment, Credit and Market Risks are among the common risk evaluations used when assessing the overall risk of an investment.

- *Investment risk:* This pertains to the possibility of default, bankruptcy and/or insolvency of the securities issuer.
- *Credit risk:* This pertains mainly to debt instruments such as bonds. Bonds are rated by credit rating agencies based on measured risk of default. The lower the collective rating by these agencies, the higher the risk of credit defaults.
- *Market risk:* This pertains to the possibility of the investment declining in value due to severe market fluctuations.
- *Interest rate risk:* This risk mainly pertains to fixed income securities. As general interest rates increase, interest rates on fixed income securities fall and inversely, as general interest rates decrease, interest rates on fixed income securities increase.
- *Currency risk:* This pertains to investments made in foreign currencies.
- Foreign currencies values are measured against the value of the U.S. dollar. Currency risk is dependent upon how the foreign currency performs against the U.S. dollar. Economic conditions are also a factor of currency risk.
- *Political risk:* This pertains to international investments and involves risk due to events such as political unrest, war and economic conditions of the country in which the investment was made.

Custodial risk: Custodial risk presents itself when deposits are made by federal agencies or governments that are uninsured and held by a financial institution, a financial institutions' trust department or held by a third party on behalf of the government or federal agency. These deposits may be either collateralized or uncollateralized, but are not held in the government or federal agencies name. These third parties are often referred to as custodians. The custodians are responsible for the safekeeping of government and federal agency deposits. The government or federal agency is exposed to custodial risk due to the possibility of the failure of the custodial institution, high administrative costs and other administrative and/or operational shortcomings of the custodial institution.

Systematic risk: Systematic risk in investments is the risk that cannot be controlled by the investor through diversification and involves the possibility of failure of an entire financial or banking system. Systematic risk is sometimes referred to as market risk and underversifiable risk. This risk is inherent in all financial systems and affects the portfolios of all financial institutions, brokerage houses and independent investors that trade investment instruments in all financial markets. The level of Systematic risk is often dependent upon the general movement of the financial markets as well as, macroeconomic changes. The value of asset classes may decline over time due to these macroeconomic and financial market changes. Systematic risk can also lead to price volatility and declining returns on investments.

Private versus public funds

Both public and private fund investments share the same three basic characteristics:

- All investors want a certain degree of safety in chosen investments. Although all investments involve risk, investors in both private and public funds should seek out investments with the goal of preserving initial investment capital.
- All investors want a certain level of liquidity. When investment decisions are being made, the degree to which the investment can be converted to cash or its' liquidity should be taken into consideration. This is important for both private and public fund investments in order to cover anticipated operating costs and other expenses.

The investors dealing with public funds have additional constraints because the higher level of accountability to the public.

- Before making an investment decision, they must often receive bids from more than one financial institution.
- They must consider the safety of an investment above all other objectives.

- Public investor may also be limited to the type of security instruments for investment and may have time constraints regarding maturity dates on investments in instruments such as money market funds, bonds and certificates of deposit.
- Public investors may also be limited to investing in only highly rated securities instruments.

Private investors are afforded more freedoms in investments in order to achieve corporate goals.
- They may be afforded a wider scope of exposure to market risk in order to achieve higher returns on investments. For instance, private investors may be able to invest in securities instruments that are not the highest rated, but offer a higher level of return due to increased credit risk.
- Private investors often do not have constraints regarding maturity dates.

Safety, liquidity and yield

The importance of Safety, Liquidity and Yield as they pertain to investment objectives:
- *Safety:* All investments involve an inherent amount of risk. Investment managers must carefully evaluate the level of safety against substantial loss each investment offers before taking action. It is very important that safety and risk are carefully evaluated in order for protection against unnecessary or avoidable losses that can adversely affect the corporations' finances.
- *Liquidity:* Refers to the ease that investments can be converted into cash. Liquidity is an important measure when evaluating investments against cash needs.
- *Yield:* Refers to the return of an investment and is often expressed in percentages using income, gains and increase in price over time as measurements. It is important to measure the return of investments against the income or gains, expected from the overall investment portfolio.

Short Term investment instruments

Short Term Investments include the following:

- *Treasury Bills:* Treasury Bills are issued and backed by the government as a way to finance debt. The benefit of T-bills is that there is virtually no risk of credit default due to the government backing.

- *Certificates of Deposit:* CD's are offered by financial institutions at a fixed rate of interest and time. The Federal Deposit Insurance Corporation backs Certificates of Deposit up to $100,000, like T-Bills, they offer virtually no risk of credit default for investments up to that amount.

- *Commercial paper:* Commercial papers are unsecured short-term promissory notes with short dates to maturity. Generally, corporation must possess high credit ratings in order to obtain commercial paper. Due to the low risk of default, commercial paper investments offer low levels of risk as compared to other investment instruments.

- *Short-term investment funds:* The pooling of funds from multiple corporations creates Short-Term Investment Funds. The combination of these funds offered the ability to meet the cash needs of corporations while at the same time, having the ability to make investments that have longer maturity dates.

Long-term investment instruments

Long-term investments are made with funds that are not marked for immediate or short-term use. Some common long-term investment instruments are the following:

- *Bonds with longer dates to maturity:* Bonds with a longer maturity date offer the bondholder less exposure to risk during market volatility and other risk measures. This allows for the bondholder to "ride out" economic downturns.

- *Zero-coupon Bonds:* These bonds do not regularly pay out interest. Instead, the interest is compounded year over year and total gains are paid out at the maturity date.

- *Equity Securities:* Equity securities are stocks, equity mutual funds and Index funds. These securities often offer a higher rate of return over a longer period of time. *Equity mutual funds* offer differing stock investments in one fund, spreading the risk associated with investing assets in only one stock. *Index funds* are funds that attempt to match the growth of stated indices. These funds offer investment in small, large and mid-cap corporations and include different classes of funds such as income, growth and value funds.

Capital Asset Pricing Model Theory

When making investment decisions, financial managers must carefully weigh the price of the investment against the risk and return. The differing theories used in making investment decisions are often collectively referred to as Capital Market Theories. Capital Asset Pricing Model theory is based in the belief that the only risk that should be considered when making investment decisions is market risk. Capital Asset Pricing Model theory asserts that market risk is the only investment risk that is out of the investors' control. Market risk, often referred to as beta, is the risk of the investment measured against the overall market. This theory is based in the belief that investors can eliminate all other investment risk through adequate diversification.

Asset allocation

Asset allocation involves the disbursement of investment funds among differing asset classes such as stock, bonds, short-term and fixed securities. These investments are to be held for a given period of time, making only minor adjustments due to market fluctuations. Spreading the funds among different asset classes is done in order to maximize return while mitigating risk. In order for a corporation or federal agency to implement asset allocation successfully, they must first decide upon the main goals and objectives of their investments as well as, decide upon what is an acceptable amount of risk. Once the goals and objectives have been determined, investment managers can strategically plan what mix of investments should be made in order to achieve the stated goals and objectives.

Investment authority

Limitations on governments and federal agencies are made in order to avoid the exposure of unnecessary or unacceptable risk pertaining to the investment of public funds. Various statutes dictate these limitations. These statutes often indicate what types of investments are acceptable, list specific financial institutions for deposits and define liquidity and collateral requirements. If these statutes dictate that a fiduciary be appointed, then the prudent person rule should be followed when making investment decisions. This rules states that the fiduciary should possess adequate knowledge of investments and act in the best interests of the government or federal agency. Governments and federal agencies may choose to outsource their investment program due to lack of experience and knowledge of investments of employees within the government or federal agency.

Investment policy

Governments and federal agencies should have written investment policies and those policies should be clearly communicated and understood by all those involved with investments and investment making decisions. Having a written policy helps to deter the mismanagement of funds and defines acceptable and unacceptable risk. Written investment policies should also clearly define the following:

- Investment objectives and goals
- Guidelines for making appropriate investment decisions
- Processes for monitoring investment performance
- Define the appropriate standards and benchmarks to be used for comparison of investments in the decision making process and in investment performance
- Regulatory compliance
- Define acceptable and unacceptable investments
- Define the responsibilities of those involved in investments and investment making decisions

Investment management controls

The most important control over investment management is that the government or federal agency is that all investments offer the collateralization of public funds. The collateralization of public funds is necessary in order to ensure the security of the federal agency or governments funds. Controls should be in place in order to ensure that all financial managers abide by all laws, rules and regulations. Periodic reviews of financial managers should be conducted in order to ascertain whether or not they are making investment decisions that are within risk guidelines. The responsibilities of money managers should be clearly defined and only individuals with adequate and proper knowledge and training should be considered for investment positions. Reporting controls should be in place dictating that financial managers submit reports that conform to applicable standards, within a defined time period that clearly describes investment performance. Finally, an independent audit should be performed in order to obtain an unbiased assessment of investment decisions and performances.

Credit Management/Debt Collection

Government credit programs

The first objective in participating in a credit program is deciding upon social and economic goals. Achieving social goals through credit programs are usually done so by giving loans. These loans include areas of increasing homeownership, providing guaranteed loans for higher education, small business loans and loans specifically geared to U.S. Military Veterans. The main difference between government loans and those offered by traditional financial institutions are that the governments' purpose for giving loans is for the forward progression of society and not to solely on making a profit. This is why some government loans are guaranteed and offered at a lower interest rate than traditional lending institutions. The second objective is Government authority. The basic premise of government authority is that the government cannot originate or collect on any loans based on terms outside what is authorized by regulatory bodies.

The governments' credit programs are mainly offered for the following reasons:

- Direct lending for credit such as student loans
- Paying on defaulted guaranteed loans
- Extending credit for the specific purpose of the purchase of governmental goods
- Services and credit extended to taxpayers that are unable or have failed to pay their taxes.

Direct Loans and Guaranteed Loans are formal government credit programs with terms and regulations dictated by legislature. Credit extension for the specific purchase of governmental goods and services and for the payment of delinquent taxes is generally offered to help individuals whom are experiencing financial hardship. Credit extension for the purchase of governmental goods arises when the debtor is experiencing financial hardship and cannot fulfill the terms of the original credit agreement. The government may restructure the original credit agreement in order for the debtor to meet its credit obligations. This concept is also applied to individuals whom are not able to meet their federal and governmental tax burdens.

Government credit programs have similar characteristics to private sector credit programs. All Government Credit Programs include the following:

- *Credit Extension:* This involves determining what applicants will receive credit and the amount of credit extended.
- *Account Servicing:* This involves determining how payments will be received and credited to the borrowers account. Account servicing also involves monitoring the borrowers account.
- *Debt Collection:* This involves collection procedures on delinquent accounts in order to bring the account current.
- *Close Out:* This involves ending the relationship between creditor and debtor.
- *Program Evaluation:* This involves evaluating the credit program in order to determine whether or not it is meeting stated goals and objectives.
- Government Credit Programs are subject to legislation regulations and requirements dictated by governing bodies such as the OMB.

Financial Management for Government credit programs -- The financial management function supports the program management function through the following activities:

- *Budget Oversight:* Financial management plans and implements the budget for credit programs.

- *Reporting:* Financial management is responsible for the periodic reporting of the credit program as well as, the reporting of expenditures.

- *Deposits and Credits:* Financial management is responsible for the deposition and crediting of funds.

- *Account Establishment:* Financial management is responsible for establishing the accounts of debtors as well as reporting payments made.

- *Credit Bureau Reporting:* Financial management is responsible for reporting the amount of the debtors' credit extension and payment history.

- *Debt Collection:* Financial management is responsible for beginning debt collection on delinquent loans and for uncollectible accounts.

Extending credit process

When offering to extend credit, businesses should first evaluate the creditworthiness of the individual. Creditworthiness is often measured by past and current payment performance on other debt obligations. It is also important to examine the amount of debt the applicant currently possesses. Examining the amount of debt an applicant is holding is an important factor in determining the ability and likelihood of repayment. This is important to ensure that the applicant will not be overextended if additional credit is granted. Corporations are obligated to adhere to the Equal Credit Opportunity Act (ECOA) regarding the extension of credit. Credit extended through federal agencies has additional criteria that must be met before granting credit. Applicants must not be delinquent in the repayment of any federal debt such as federal taxes and guaranteed loans such as student loans. Additionally, if an applicant owes back child support federal agencies will deny the extension of credit.

Internal controls should be in place to ensure the proper documenting and reporting procedures of granting credit and specific guidelines should be in place and communicated to all individuals involved in the extension of credit. Periodic audits of loans granted should be performed in order to ensure that all individuals are complying with ECOA laws and regulations as well as credit extension guidelines.

Periodic audits also ensure that when credit is granted, there are no conflicts of interest and that all documentation is complete, legal and accurate. Internal controls regarding communication when extending credit should also be in place. The helps to ensure that credit decisions are not made based on an individuals' subjective judgment and in the case where exceptions to guidelines are made, that approvals are received from the appropriate manager or executive.

Account servicing process

Successful account servicing begins with building a positive working relationship between the finance office staff and program staff. A positive work relationship is important because there is a lot of face-to-face communication involved in the account servicing process. Establishing a positive working relationship helps to ensure that all tasks are completely in a timely fashion. Both program and finance staff must also regularly communicate the amount of money that is available for each program. Next, the program staff must provide adequate information to the finance staff when establishing new accounts. This ensures that there are no delays in receipt of funds for the debtor and allows for the finance office to monitor the debtors' account performance and gather and maintain information for audit purposes.

- *Methods of receiving funds:* Both finance and program departments must decide upon the varying ways to receive payments. The payment methods should be beneficial to the responsibilities of both departments.
- *Crediting accounts:* When a payment has been made, both departments should ensure that the associated account is credited properly and in a timely manner.
- *Monitoring credit and reporting:* Both departments are responsible for monitoring credit performance and deciding upon what actions are to be taken if it is found that the debtor is not fulfilling the terms of the credit agreement.

- *Negotiating delinquencies:* If a serious delinquency is found to occur with some degree of frequency, the program staff is responsible for discussing and re-negotiating the terms of the credit agreement in order to satisfy any delinquencies.
- *Credit bureau reporting:* The finance office is responsible for the reporting of credit extension to the credit bureaus.
- *Measuring portfolio risk*: Risk to the overall portfolio should be adequately measured using the appropriate risk measurement models.

Evaluating credit programs

Credit programs are often divided into 2 categories for evaluation purposes.

The first category involves assessing whether or not the program is meeting its' stated goals and objectives.

The second category involves assessing debt collection procedures and activities.

The periodic evaluation of credit programs allows for the discovery of material weaknesses or deficiencies in the program. If these weaknesses or deficiencies are discovered, changes can then be made and implemented to the program before the problems compound. An integral part to any credit program is evaluating debt collection procedures for effectiveness and efficiency. If the debt collection activities and procedures are found ineffective or inefficient, changes can be implemented in order to more successfully collect debt before it becomes uncollectible and must be written off.

Delinquent debt collection

Methods of collecting on delinquent debt:
- *Dunning Procedures:* These procedures involve sending a series of letters to the debtor regarding the delinquency. Each subsequent letter should include wording of increased urgency regarding the debt, then the previous letter.
- *Administrative Offset:* Delinquent payments are offset by charging deposit accounts or other future payments from any federal agency to the debtor from other credit accounts.
- *Salary Offset:* A percentage of delinquent payments may be withheld from wages if the debtor is an employee.

- *Collection Agencies:* Private Collection Agencies may be contracted by the creditor in order to collect on delinquent payments.
- *Asset Sales*: A sale of assets may be authorized for any non-tax debt owed that is more than 90 days old.

Procedures regarding delinquent debt:
- *Referral:* Any federal debt that is more than 180 days old may be referred to the U.S. Department of Treasury for further review and collection.
- *Tax refund offset:* Any future tax refunds expected by the debtor may be used as payment toward any delinquent accounts.
- *Uncollectible debt:* If it is determined that the outstanding delinquent debt is uncollectible, and then steps must be taken to remove the debt from current accounting books and close the delinquent account.
- *Referral for litigation*: The delinquent account may be referred for litigation for further collection procedures.
- *Write off:* If an account is 2 or more years past due, all collection attempts have been exhausted and there is no reason to believe that the delinquent payments will be recovered; the account must then be written off.

Debt write-offs

The Treasury Department dictates that all debt that is over 2 years old must be written off. The federal agency may consult with the OMB or Department of Treasury regarding the justification by the federal agency for debt that is not written off in that time period. Federal agencies that extend credit are required to have an allowance fund for debt write offs and all write offs are to be processed through this account and are never to be processed directly to expense. Once written off, the agency must determine whether the debt is to be classified as currently not collectible or if the account is to be closed out. Collection activities on written off debt are to continue unless the agency determines that the benefits no longer outweigh the costs to continue such efforts.

Evaluation of credit programs and debt-collection

The two main objectives of credit program evaluation are to first evaluate whether or not the program is meeting its' stated goals and second to evaluate whether or not it is effectively collecting debt. The following measures are used in program evaluation:

- *Activity measures:* Evaluate the amount the total amount of loans originated, the total number and dollar amount of loans outstanding, amount of payments received and evaluating all exception items.
- *Status measures:* These measure evaluate the number and dollar amount of delinquent accounts, the age of delinquent accounts, number and dollar amounts of write offs and assets that have been seized.
- *Efficiency measures:* Measures the costs to the benefits of the program.
- *Effectiveness measures:* Evaluate whether or not debt collection methods are effective.

Management should effectively monitor all debt collectors and their activities in order to ensure that these activities comply with the Fair Debt Collection Practices Act (FDCPA). This can be accomplished by first properly training and communicating the FDCPA to all debt collectors within the agency. Management should periodically evaluate debt collectors and their activities through observation. Examining financial statements may also be a helpful tool in monitoring debt collection activities. This allows for management to evaluate whether current debt collection practices are economic and efficient by comparing the dollar amounts of debt collected to the costs of the debt collection activities. If the amount of debt collected is low relative to the costs of debt collection activities, management may determine that the debt collection activities be changed in order to become more cost efficient and effective.

Program management

The main objectives and goals for government credit programs are determined and defined through legislation. Program management involves the following factors:

- *Credit eligibility:* Program personnel must follow all requirements when determining a credit applicant's eligibility.

- *Credit extension amounts:* Program personnel must follow the established maximum credit extension amounts as dictated by legislation. Lesser amounts of credit may be extended at the agencies discretion dependent upon the debtors' eligibility.
- *Terms and conditions:* Program personnel must follow the general term and conditions of credit extension dictated by legislation. The federal agency must dictate additional terms and condition requirements.
- *Repayment:* Payments on outstanding loans must be monitored by the agency. The agency is solely responsible for collecting payments on outstanding loans.
- *Negotiation:* Program personnel are responsible for payment arrangements and other workout programs offered in cases of a debtors' inability of repayment according to the original terms of the loan. Overall guidelines of these programs are dictated by legislation and developed in detail by the federal agency.

Direct versus guaranteed loan

Direct loans given by the government or a federal agency are loans to non-federal borrowers to be paid back over a given time period. The government or federal agency may or may not charge interest to direct loan borrowers depending on the type of direct loan. A common example of direct loans given by the government is federal student loans. Direct loans given by non-governmental financial institutions are loans given to the borrower through a third party lender, broker or financial institution.

Guaranteed loans are given by a traditional lender or financial institution where all, or a portion of, the loan is guaranteed by the government if the borrower does not fulfill the terms of the loan or defaults on the loan through non-payment.

Procurement Management

The main objectives regarding procurement are making sure that the appropriate dollar amounts are paid for products and services. The specific needs of the product and/or service should be determined before any goods or services are procured. This ensures that they equally match needs in quality and/or quantity. The risks of procurement management involve:

- Paying too much for a good or service
- Failures by outside sources such as suppliers or vendors
- The specific needs of the good or service have not been determined
- Failures in the any of the processes or acquiring goods and services
- Procuring sub-par goods or services

Specifications process

When establishing specifications for procurement it is important that these specifications contain enough detail so that contractors, vendors and suppliers can appropriately bid on the good or service required. If the specifications are vague, this can lead to unnecessary increases in cost, the inability to hold the contractors, vendors or suppliers responsible for their goods or services and unnecessary delays. During the planning and coordinating phases of procurement, it is important that all relevant parties openly communicate their specific needs completely regarding the good and or service to be procured. This ensures that all needs of the involved parties are met and there is no confusion due to miscommunication.

Establishing specifications help to keep costs within an acceptable range and encourage competitive bidding from various vendors, contractors and suppliers. Some important considerations when developing specifications for procurement are the following:

- When relevant parties are establishing specifications, there should be a point in the process where they are required to "freeze" their specifications. This ensures that bidders are giving appropriate up-to-date estimates for costs.
- When establishing specifications for services needed the duties expected should be detailed enough to hold the contractors responsible for meeting the terms of the agreement.

- All specifications should not involve favoritism toward any one contractor, vendor and/or supplier. This encourages competitive bidding.
- Guidelines of the Federal Acquisition Regulation should be followed.
- All operating costs after the project is completed should be given full consideration.

Risk considerations: If the federal agency fails to develop and implement the specifications in procurement, it can lead to costly delays in contract performance and excessive costs in the administrative process. When federal agencies do not specify what is needed and what is expected of the contractor, it runs the risk of time and cost overruns. These time and cost overruns can lead to major budgetary planning and forecasting issues for the federal agency. In the goal toward establishing detailed specifications, the federal agency should take care not to provide an unnecessary amount of detail. This may lead to the shrinking of the competitive base, therefore, discouraging competitive bidding. If competitive bidding is discouraged, the federal agency will fail to achieve the overall goal of obtaining the needed good or service for the proper and acceptable price.

Planning phase
- Defining the project
- Establishing budgets and budgetary guidelines
- Conducting feasibility studies and reviewing funding issues

Specifications should be properly and adequately planned by considering all the components involved in the procurement of a good or service. During the planning phase, federal agencies should consider viable alternatives to new procurement or construction, conduct a thorough cost benefit analysis and evaluate the environment in which the good or service will be put to use. Larger procurement projects such as major construction projects involve extensive planning that can involve various federal agencies and private sector companies. The proper planning in the procurement process helps to ensure the success of the goods of services to be provided.

Coordination phase:

Extensive procurement projects involve a large number of various personnel, federal agencies and private sector companies. In such cases, it may be necessary to establish a project team comprised of personnel from different departments of the federal agency. A project manager should be appointed in order to coordinate meetings between relevant varying agencies, departments and private sector companies in order to successfully communicate the procurement plan goals, objectives, provide a timeframe in which the specification process is to be completed, as well as, address the needs of all parties involved. At this time, budgetary guidelines and expected timelines toward the completion of the project should be communicated and discussed. Periodic meetings should also be conducted in order to inform relevant parties as to the progress of the project or any possible or existing problems.

Goods and services suppliers

One of the first decisions often made when obtaining suppliers for goods and services is whether or not it would be more cost efficient to outsource the work. This involves completing an in depth cost analysis as well as performing feasibility studies. The cost analyses and feasibility studies should involve considering the costs of a non-government agency performing the service and other issues outside of cost that may affect the performance of the service. The next consideration is to review any requirements of competition due to laws and regulations. The total cost of resources used during the procurement process should also be taken into consideration. This includes any administrative costs and the total cost of time spent on the procurement process.

Risks with soliciting and selecting suppliers: A good deal of consideration should be given to controlling the risks associated with the procurement process. Controlling these risks will help keep costs within reasonable limits. When the need for a good or service is established, agencies should make sure that a sufficient amount of suppliers have been solicited in order to receive the best price for the good or service to be provided. If this does not occur, then the agency risks increased costs for the good or service to be provided. It is also important that all laws and regulations regarding competition are followed. If they aren't, this can lead to costly fines or delays.

Finally, the easiest and most cost efficient method of procurement should be used first. This ensures that costs are kept at a minimum when possible.

Outsourcing

A government or federal agency may decide to outsource a service or the production of an item to corporations in the private sector. Outsourcing is generally done when it is more cost efficient for the government or federal agency. Before making the decision to outsource, governments and federal agencies must conduct a thorough cost-benefit analysis as well as, conduct feasibility studies. This allows for the determination of whether it is more beneficial to outsource when all costs are considered. When considering the costs to include in the cost benefit analysis, only the costs that can be improved upon or reduced should be considered. Also included, should be the possibility of new costs that may be incurred when contracting private sector corporations. Feasibility studies should include all other relevant issues outside of cost such as service quality and security issues.

Simplifying the procurement process

The procurement process is often time consuming and involves many different administrative costs. There are prescribed steps that can be taken in order to reduce time and cost elements. The following are common methods of practice toward the reduction of overall procurement costs:

- *Buying from statewide and federal contracts:* It is common for state governments to have statewide contracts for commonly used supplies and equipment. These statewide contracts offer the federal agency price discounts by buying the items in bulk. The General Services Administration catalog is also a good tool for making bulk purchases.
- *Blanket purchase agreements:* These agreements dictate that bulk contracts of governments cover a specific time period.
- *Small purchase procedures:* Small purchases of up to $10,000 may be conducted through the use of receiving 3 telephone bids. Larger purchases cannot be broken up into smaller quantities in order to meet the criteria of Small Purchase Procedures.

- *Credit cards:* Governments and federal agencies may obtain commercial credit cards and designate authorized users to pay for goods and services within the designated spending limits.

Emergency procurements

From time to time, the need for an emergency procurement may arise due to previously unforeseen events or occurrences such as natural disasters. In order to prevent price gouging or favoritism, the following are common requirements for emergency procurement procedures:

- *Maintaining a list of pre-qualified contractors:* This is useful because the contractor is already qualified to do the work required and has a proven track record.
- *Seeking proposals within a specified time from after the emergency has occurred:* This helps ensure that the goods or services required will be delivered or performed within an acceptable period of time.
- *Receiving proposals from a specified number of contractors:* By keeping the specified number of contractors bidding on the project, competition regulations will still be upheld with minimal time consumption.

Ensuring competition during bidding

Governments and federal agencies will help to ensure competition during the bidding process by adhering to Federal Acquisition Act regulations and procedures for broadening and strengthening the competitive base. Utilizing a wide range of mediums for advertising the federal agencies needs, will help to reach a wider range of contracting companies for the good or service required. Federal agencies may want to look beyond the scope of traditional government wide print and website advertisements and include local and national print and electronic advertisements. Federal agencies may also want to determine the number of bids relative to the size and scope of the goods or services needed that are sufficient enough to be deemed fairly competitive.

Legal requirements regarding competition

All federal agencies must adhere to the regulations of the Federal Acquisition Act during the procurement process. This act states that all federal agencies must promote an open competition and solicitation process for contractors bidding on government projects and establishes uniform practices in which all governments and federal agencies must adhere. The open competition and solicitation process should be conducive to meeting the needs of the federal agency while promoting fairness in competition. The Federal Acquisition act is necessary in order to efficiently and effectively promote competition, keep administrative costs to a minimum, to operate within the guidelines of public policy while keeping the best interests of the government, federal agency and general public.

Broadening and expanding the competitive base

By having a wide array of competitive bids on contracts helps to ensure that federal agencies are receiving the best price for the work to be completed. The following steps can be taken to broaden and expand a competitive base:

- Laws require governments to advertise their procurement needs through the Internet, government publications and newspapers. This ensures that procurement needs reach a large amount of contracting companies.
- Accessing bidder's lists maintained by federal agencies.
- Gathering information on contracting companies and suppliers from other governments.
- Utilizing a pre-qualification process of contractor selection that includes past performance history, backgrounds on all relevant employees and the company's financial ability to complete the contract work successfully.

Contracts

The basic elements of a contract should include:

- The total payment to the contractor for the good or service provided. This will vary dependant upon the type of contract written.
- The quality of work expected and the quantity of goods to be produced.
- Should include all allowable and unallowable costs should be clearly stated.
- The time frame in which the work is expected to be completed and delivery dates should also be clearly stated.

- Any penalties or consequences for late delivery or delays in work completion should be discussed by all parties and included in the terms of the contract.
- All insurance requirements, warranties and labor laws should be included in the terms of the contract as well.

Fixed price contracts are contracts in which the prices cannot be changed. The terms of the contract remain fixed throughout the contract period. Authorized personnel can make changes to Fixed Price contracts if the scope or needs of the services contracted changes. Fixed price contracts allow for federal agencies and the contractor to set the price of the contract before work begins in an effort to avoid budget overruns. The contractor knows before the project begins what services are expected of the company and the level of the quality of service or product is expected in return, the federal agency knows exactly what type of service and quality of service that is expected from the contractor. Having these specifications helps to deter unethical practices or poor workmanship on the contractors' part.

A *cost-type contract* is a contract that specifies what are considered allowable and unallowable payments for a good or service provided. Cost type contracts are utilized when there is difficulty establishing prices or specific requirements pertaining to the good or service that is to be provided. A set limit of the amount of allowable costs should be established in order to ensure that the contract will be fulfilled within budgetary guidelines. If these costs are not established, this may lead the contractor to have less incentive on controlling costs during contract performance, leaving the federal agency exposed to significant cost risks. It is beneficial for the federal agency to conduct audits of allowable costs during the performance phase of the contract in order to ensure that the costs are staying within stated specifications.

- *Cost plus a fixed fee contract:* Contracts that specifically detail the contractor fee and determines additional acceptable and allowable costs.
- *Cost plus an incentive fee contract:* Contracts that specifies the contractor fee as well as allowable costs. The contractor fee in these types of contract varies and is directly related to the amount of allowable costs.

- *Cost with no fee:* Contracts that specifies allowable fees for which the contractor will be reimbursed.
- *Cost sharing contracts:* Contracts in which both the contractor and federal agency shares the cost and the contractor does not receive a fee.
- *Time and material contracts:* Contract is which a flat fee is established for per hour or per day work and includes the costs for materials and supplies.

The main points of *monitoring contract performance* are:
- *Risk:* Major risks are excess contractor costs, significant changes in the contract due to any problems that may arise, errors in contractor billing and the quality or quantity of the good or service delivered is less than specified.
- *Timeliness of delivery:* Contractors may deliver goods or services late.
- *Quantity delivered:* The contractor or vendor may deliver the wrong amount of goods.
- *Costs and billing:* Accounting systems and controls should be in place in order to ensure that contractors are not paid for the same services more than once. Also, if the specifications of the contract or changed, the agency may run into cost overruns due to these necessary changes.

Inventory/Supply management

The main objective to Inventory supply management is to ensure the proper and adequate safeguarding of inventories and supplies. Proper inventory supply management ensures that governments and federal agencies have an adequate amount of inventory available so as not to have too much or too little. Overages and shortages have the tendency to increase the overall costs attributable to the inventories and supplies. Another main objective to inventory supply management is for the protection against loss due to theft, spoilage, deterioration and obsolescence. A final major objective and goal of Inventory Supply Management is to establish and maintain accountability for inventories and supplies until time of use or disposition due to obsolescence or loss due to breakage, spoilage or deterioration.

Inventory supply management risk

The most obvious risks to inventory supply management are either having too much inventory or too little inventory. Not having a sufficient amount of inventory poses the problem of supply not meeting demand. This leads to the inability for the federal agency to achieve its' stated goals and objectives. Having too much inventory increases the costs of a federal agency or program and also leads to the inability to achieve stated goals due to the increased costs. Finally, a major risk in inventory supply management is risk of loss due to spoilage, theft or if the inventory becomes obsolete before it is used. Due to these risks, inventory supply managers should develop and implement an inventory supply system that provides the proper balance between having too much inventory and having too little.

Maintaining government inventories

Just as with any business or corporation, federal agencies have large quantities of inventories. Just as with any business or corporation, federal agencies inventory must be adequately maintained. Federal agencies maintain inventories in order to exchange or sell them to other agencies or units with in the government. Government inventories must also be maintained in order to determine the replacement or repair of current inventory such as public service vehicles and military equipment and hardware. Government inventories also include items such as highways and sewage and water mains. The maintenance of these types of inventories is necessary in determining needed repairs and physical maintenance of these structures. Inventories must also be managed regarding the consumption of products such as public school supplies and for stockpiling in the event of a national emergency or disaster.

Inventory systems

Components – The main components of an inventory system are deciding when and how much inventory should be ordered and delivered and how that inventory is to be received, stored and utilized. With smaller corporations and federal agencies, both these components can be achieved without making use of perpetual inventory accounting methods. This is done by either estimating the amount of inventory needed or by ordering based on past history. For larger organizations however, the large scope of goods offered and the consequent cost of ordering and warehousing the inventory necessitates the need for perpetual inventory accounting methods. Finally, inventory systems should provide the authorized dollar amount to be spent on acquiring new inventory, the condition of the inventory and controls in place to prevent theft, obsolescence and spoilage.

Major functions:

- The *supply control function* is necessary to determine the current amount of inventory and the amount of inventory to re-order and the time in which inventory should b re-ordered. The supply control function is also necessary when assessing consumer needs and in determining inventory costs.
- The *inventory control function* is necessary to adequately process, receive and warehouse inventories. This function also determines the steps that are to be taken when disposing of inventory. The inventory control function is also necessary for the protection against loss, spoilage and theft. Finally, this function is necessary to ensure that physical inventory amounts match stated inventory amounts.

Supply management

Supply control – The main goal of supply control is to ensure that there are enough inventories on hand to meet consumer demand. In order to consistently meet consumer demand, inventory supply managers must meet with consumers in order to discuss the consumers' needs regarding quantities of inventory required and the time frame in which they are needed.

Inventory managers must also be aware of the proper time in which inventories are to be reordered. This helps to prevent costly inventory overages and shortages. Finally, inventory supply managers must know the quantity of inventories to be ordered while taking both administrative and ordering costs into consideration. Administrative costs are the costs incurred for ordering and warehousing the inventory and costs associated with stolen or damaged inventories. Ordering costs are the costs incurred for the actual purchase, shipping and delivery of inventories.

Inventory control activities

- *Receiving and inspecting:* All inventories received must be inspected in order to ensure what has been delivered matches what was ordered. Receiving and inspecting inventories is also necessary to ensure that the proper amount has been delivered.

- *Placing in inventory:* Once the inventories have been inspected they must stored in an area that is readily accessible such as a warehouse. When necessary, inventories should be labeled for ownership and security purposes. Information regarding the monetary values of the inventories delivered should also be recorded and maintained.

- *Movement and tracking:* When inventory is physically moved, that movement must be recorded. Also, inventory movement that is done in order to prevent loss from breakage, spoilage or theft should also be recorded and tracked.

- *Accounting for stored Items:* An accurate physical count on all inventories in storage should be maintained and recorded. An accurate record of any inventory that is lost due to damage, spoilage obsolescence or theft should also be maintained.

- *Issuance and other disposition:* An accurate record of the use and/or sale of the inventories should be maintained and any discrepancies regarding the amounts of inventories should be recorded.

- *Accounting for Items in transit:* Information on all inventories that are in transit either to a storage facility or to the end user should be accurately recorded or maintained.

- *Inventory undergoing repair or in production:* Information on all inventories currently under production and inventories being repaired should be accurately recorded and maintained.

- *Policy and procedures manuals:* Specific guidelines and processes regarding inventories should be clearly defined in the policy and procedures manual. All employee and management responsibilities regarding inventories should be clearly defined and communicated. All inventory activities and transactions where management approval is necessary should also be clearly defined.

- *Separation of duties:* The expected duties of employees and management regarding inventories activities should be clearly defined and communicated. This helps to deter act of collusion, theft and fraudulent activities not only internally, but also externally as well.

- *Ensuring inspection accuracy:* All inspectors should receive proper and adequate training in order to effectively complete accurate inventory inspections as well as accurate physical inventory counts.

- *Storage:* Adequate training and monitoring should be provided in order to ensure that inventories are properly stored. Inventories that have a specific shelf life should be stored in a first-in first-out manner in order to prevent loss due to spoilage or the physical deterioration of the items. Any inventory losses due to spoilage or deterioration should be accurately accounted for.

- *Safeguarding:* Inventories should be accessed by only authorized personnel, tagged for ownership and kept in a securely locked area when necessary.

- *Physical verification:* A physical inventory account of items in storage should take place as often as the federal agency or corporation dictates, but no less than once a year. The current physical counts should be compared to the perpetual inventory records. Physical verification is necessary to detect cases of fraud, theft and collusion, but also in order to determine whether or not inventory shortages and overages have occurred. This also allows relevant personnel, such as the inventory supply manager to determine the overall condition of the inventory and whether or not it has become obsolete.

Safeguarding inventories

The best way the inventories and supplies can be safeguarded is to effectively implement internal controls over inventories and supplies. The consistent and ongoing monitoring and reporting of inventories and supplies also help to ensure their safeguarding.

All transactions regarding the procurement, delivery, warehousing and returns and/or repairs to inventories and supplies should be documented and reported in a timely manner. Employee responsibilities and job duties regarding the handling of inventories and supplies should be clearly communicated, acknowledged and understood by all employees. Management should clearly dictate and communicate the consequences for the unethical or illegal behavior of employees such as, stealing or collusion. It is important that if these instances should occur that management follow through with any disciplinary actions.

Administrative lead time

Administrative Lead Time is the amount of time between when the order is taken from the consumer and when the inventory or supplies are delivered. Supply managers must be aware of the administrative lead-time in order to ensure that the proper amount of inventory is ordered and received in a timely and cost efficient manner. The supply manager should also be mindful of changes in consumer demand that may lead to longer administrative lead times. In this event, the inventory supply manager should consider the costs and benefits of storing additional inventories in the case that such an event occurs. These considerations should also be evaluated for unforeseen events such as problems with suppliers, vendors and shippers.

Inventory reporting

The major objectives to inventory supply and control reporting:

- The first major objective to inventory supply and control reporting is to ensure that internal controls over inventories and supplies are effective.
- Inventory supply and control reporting allows for management to keep an accurate physical amount and an accurate monetary value of inventories and supplies.
- This reporting also allows for the prevention of costly stock shortages and overages.
- The ongoing monitoring of inventories and supplies also aids in the early detection and deterrence of theft and collusion either among employees or among employees and suppliers.
- Finally, the stocking, warehousing and ordering of inventories can be costly. These costs range from administrative costs to the costs of raw materials. By conducting ongoing monitoring activities and keeping accurate reports of these activities, this allows for federal agencies and corporations to help keep these costs under control.

<u>Inventory and supply management reports</u>

Inventory and supply reports are useful for monitoring and controlling activities of inventories and supplies. The following are common reports used in controlling activities:

- *Dollar amount of unfilled orders:* This report shows the amount of orders that are waiting to be filled and the dollar value of those unfilled orders.
- *Days supply on hand:* Shows the estimated time when the current supply will run out.
- *Budget versus actual:* Shows the actual amount of supplies compared to the budgeted amount of supplies.
- *Inactive, excess and obsolete stock:* All supplies that fall into these 3 categories should be included in this report and the reason why the inventory has become inactive, in excess or obsolete should be investigated and documented.
- *Breakage and spoilage:* All cases of breakage and spoilage should be investigated and documented.
- *Out of stock instances:* This report should include a comparison of the amount of orders requested to the amount of stock on hand to fill the orders. When orders cannot be filled due to shortages and outages in stock, the reasons should be investigated and reported.
- *Periodic user surveys:* These questionnaires allow for an unbiased opinion of the management of the supply system and allow for management to adjust controls if deficiencies or weaknesses are discovered.
- *Inventory difference ratio:* Physical inventories should be taken and compared against the perpetual inventory records in order to account for shortages and overages. The dollar value of the shortages or overages should be reported.
- *Inventory turnover ratio:* This report measures the time in which it takes to move inventory.

Financial management systems

<u>Goals</u>

The overall goal of financial management systems is to monitor and control financially related events and activities of the federal agency. Financial systems are necessary for the preparation of agency budgets, the overall financial planning of the agency and financial statements and reporting.

Ensuring that all financial information regarding financial events, statements, reports and budgets are recorded accurately and in a timely manner is also a main goal of financial management systems. These systems also allow for federal agencies to more effectively manage capital assets and monitor spending. Additional goals for financial management systems are to provide audit information, supporting documentation for policy and budgetary decision-making as well as to provide information for performance measurement.

JFMIP guidelines

The Joint Financial Management Improvement Program for the Federal Government has issued the following guidelines regarding the composition of financial management systems:

- *Overall system management*: The system should include components that classify accounts and have controls over financial transactions.
- *General ledger management:* The system should include components regarding the management of the general ledger.
- *Funds management:* The system should include components regarding the management of funds in areas of budgets, resource allocation and control over resources and assets.
- *Receivables management:* The system should include the necessary components in order to effectively manage receivables, customer information and debt and credit activity.
- *Payables management:* The system should include the necessary components of effectively manages all payments and payment information.
- *Cost management:* The system should include the necessary components to effectively and efficiently manage costs and working capital.
- *Management over reporting:* The system should include components necessary to ensure that all internal and external reporting is reliable, accurate and timely.

Financial management COTS products -- COTS are commercial off the shelf products. Federal agencies and corporations often purchase and use these products because they are mass produced and readily available. COTS financial management systems are purchased because they are often less costly than planning, developing and implementing a brand new financial management system. The major downfall to COTS products is that federal agencies and corporations rarely find one product that fits all the needs of the agency. When this occurs, modifications to the product must be made in order to be implemented efficiently and effectively utilized. Any cost savings realized in the purchase of the COTS product may be negated dependent upon the level of modifications that must be made. Before purchasing a commercial off the shelf financial management system, the financial manager must fully understand and comprehend the financial management needs of the agency. All system requirements of the various users of the financial management system should be clearly defined and discussed before the financial management system is purchased. This helps to ensure that the needs of the main departments involved will be met. It is often found that no single COTS product fits all the needs and requirements of the agency. That being the case, the agency should consider the possibility of combining existing financial management systems with newly acquired systems. It should be noted that combining both systems is not recommended, as it tends to increase the overall costs of the financial management system.

Key considerations

Some of the same considerations are given to developing a Financial Management System and purchasing a COTS Financial Management System such as the full comprehension of the needs of the agency and defining and discussing the varying needs of different departments within the agency. Financial managers must successfully communicate these needs to the department in charge of developing the actual financial management system. Generally, the main goals of developing a new financial management system are to increase efficiency and to meet growing and varying needs. Financial managers and developers must keep these goals in mind when designing new financial management systems in order to avoid repeating activities that are no longer relevant and/or have become inefficient.

Implementation

Implementing new financial management systems is often a cumbersome and time-consuming task because:

- All the information and data from the previous financial management system must be transferred and converted to the new financial management system.
- During the implementation phase, financial managers and those involved should reassess business processes and remove all processes that are no longer valid or provide no added value.
- When implementing a new financial management system, care should be taken to communicate all the components of the new systems with the system users. If this communication does not take place, it may lead to unnecessary mistakes by users and increased costs due to these mistakes.
- Proper and thorough training should be provided to all personnel regarding the new financial management system in order for it to be implemented successfully.
- Finally, before putting the new system to use, the financial management system should be carefully evaluated in order to ensure that it meets all the needs and requirements of the agency.

Internal control components

Internal controls over financial management systems are necessary to safeguard assets, ensure that all information in financial reporting is accurate and reliable and for performance measurement reporting. The five general internal control components of Control Environment:

- Risk assessment
- Control activities
- Information
- Communication
- Monitoring

These all apply to financial management systems. These general internal controls should be applied to financial management and financial management systems with the goals of ensuring all financial information and transactions are recorded accurately and in a timely fashion, ensuring that all assets are adequately safeguarded from loss, misuse, abuse and fraud and all financial information is reliable and truthful. Separate audits of financial management systems should be conducted in order to evaluate the efficacy of internal controls over financial management systems.

Evaluation components

The regular and ongoing monitoring of financial management systems is necessary in order to assess whether or not the systems are meeting requirements and objectives and that the systems are operating in the manner in which they were designed. During the course of the evaluations, officials should compare the previous financial system processes with the current system processes in order to determine whether or not the desired goals of implementing the new system have occurred. Officials should also conduct tests regarding whether or not the users have successfully accepted and implemented the new financial management systems. All data that is gathered during the evaluation of financial management systems should be quantified in order to adequately measure its' level of successes and failures.

Single integrated management system

A financial management system includes all information related to the processing, maintaining, and preparation of financial statements and reporting of all financially related activities. A financial management system is also used in fiscal and budgetary planning. The financial management system allows for the monitoring of internal controls over financial activities. A single integrated financial management system is a system that combines financial information and activities as well as, non-financial activities and information that contributes to the management of financial functions. All single integrated financial management systems in federal agencies must comply with OMB and Department of Treasury requirements. Having a single integrated financial management system is more cost effective, helps to prevent cases of fraud or abuse and allows for internal controls over financial management to be monitored more efficiently.

Public procurement process

Authorized procurement official, compiling a bidders list, and public advertising

1. Authorized Procurement Official: This is someone who has been designated specifically to issue purchase orders and to coordinate purchases. Only those with this designation are allowed to initiate purchases on the behalf of the government.
2. Compiling a bidder's list: Before the procurement official can initiate the purchase, it must be determined who the government will be contracting with. This is done by compiling a list of bids and determining who can fulfill the order at the lowest price.
3. Public Advertising: In the past, the government has been criticized for not publicly advertising that they were accepting bids on a contract, and as a result, only those who were in the inner circle knew in time to submit a bid. Publicly advertising that bids are being accepted is now a standard practice.

Issuing an invitation to bid (ITB) and a request for proposal (RFP)

1. An invitation to bid (ITB) also is known as a formal competitive solicitation in the form of a sealed bid. Once all sealed bids have been received, the results are publicly posted to foster transparency with the public.
2. A request for proposal (RFP) is the way in which a government (or company) announces that funding is available for a particular project, good, or service and that companies are invited to submit a bid to be involved.

Ensuring contract efficiency in the procurement process

1. A purchase card (also known as a P-Card) is a company (or government) charge card that allows for goods and services to be purchased without going through an official purchasing process. In other words, instead of filling out a purchase order, the holder of the purchase card goes straight to the vender and purchases the item as a point-of-sale purchase.
2. Bulk purchasing allows for companies (and governments) to pay less on a per-item basis by agreeing to buy a large quantity of the item. This allows the company to benefit from economies of scale.
3. Interagency procurements: At times it is not necessary for an agency to purchase an item straight from the vender. Instead, the agency gets the item from another agency that has overstocked the item and transfers the cost internally.

Enterprise resource planning (ERP) system

Enterprise resource planning (ERP) is a business process management software system that allows businesses to automate many of their functions rather than having an actual person perform the tasks. Examples of this include the generation of reports that previously would have been compiled by a member of the staff. The cost of the system may be large up front, but a break-even analysis demonstrates that over time, the company can save money by freeing up staff to work on other tasks that cannot be automated or by employing fewer people overall.

Continuity of operations plan

A continuity of operations plan is similar to a business continuity plan, only it is specifically for government agencies. The idea is that the US government should still be able to function in the face of very difficult circumstances and requires a written plan documenting what would need to occur to ensure the government could respond to a broad range of circumstances including war, acts of terrorism, natural disasters, and massive power outages.

Different aspects of project management, defining interrelationships, cost and schedule control, and cost and performance management

1. Interrelationships: A team approach is required to meet the goals of the project. This term means that before someone can complete a task or a project, another individual must perform an action or complete a task of his or her own. Specific deadlines and time lines must be created to ensure that large tasks are tackled in the right order.
2. Cost and Schedule Control: Projects generally have a firm cost and schedule associated with them. In most cases, staying within the confines of cost and schedule is of vital importance. However, in some cases, the time line for completion will be moved up, requiring additional funding. Alternatively, if the budget for a project is cut, the schedule may have to be adjusted to account for the loss of head count.
3. Performance Management: Performance management is an important part of project management, particularly for long-term projects, as people will need regular feedback to make course corrections to ensure completion and quality of results.

Meeting system needs

1. Off the Shelf: A company is purchasing a system that was designed by a third party to meet the needs of the masses. Sometimes this is beneficial because it can be implemented quickly. However, in other cases, using an off-the-shelf product is not plausible because it will not meet the specific intricacies and needs of the people.

2. Cross Servicing: This is a way to share costs among departments, organizations, and agencies. If there is a need that is shared among groups, developing or purchasing a system to accommodate all requests can be very practical.
3. Outsourcing: This is a way to avoid purchasing or developing systems altogether. Rather than performing a task internally, a company or agency will hire an external firm to handle it. Common examples are benefits outsourcing and IT outsourcing.

Using forensic techniques

To get ahead of trends or predict the next big thing, many companies will use forensic techniques such as data mining. Data mining is a technique that allows a business to analyze meta data such as customer demographics, purchase trends, and other distinct patterns to make key decisions, validate findings, and decide how and where to invest profits. This allows companies to have more conclusive data on which to make decisions.

Standards set by the Government Accountability Office

The Government Accountability Office (GAO) was created to help improve the performance of the federal government and provide information to Congress that is fair, balanced, and nonpartisan. They do this in the following ways:
1. Auditing agency operations to see if they are using the funds allocated to them in an effective and efficient manner
2. Investigating allegations of illegal or unethical activities
3. Reporting on whether (or how well) government programs are meeting their stated objectives
4. Performing policy analysis
5. Issuing legal decisions and opinions, particularly to bid protest rulings

Sensitive government audit activities

During government audits, auditors are given access to information that is considered particularly sensitive including taxpayer data, payments to informants, and patient information protected under the Health Insurance Portability and Accountability Act (HIPAA). As a result, auditors are required to sign nondisclosure documents promising to keep the information secure, must use encryption software when transmitting any data, and in some cases are required to be HIPAA certified. In addition, it is understood that using personal or private information in any way other than as attended will result in criminal prosecution and large fines.

Performance Measurement and Reporting

Performance measurement

Objectives – Performance measurements are used to evaluate whether or not the corporation or federal agency is achieving its' stated or expected goals. Expected goals are measured against the actual performance of the corporation to determine whether the corporation is achieving or progressing toward these goals. Before a performance measurement evaluation begins, a plan must be defined and specific areas of performance evaluation are to be determined. This is done in order to ensure that relevant areas are being reviewed and time and resources are not wasted in measuring irrelevant subjects. Common subjects to review for performance measurements include: Financial data, public perception, overall business activities and employee performance and satisfaction levels. Evaluating performance measurements also provides the opportunity for management to review stated and expected goals and to determine whether those goals remain relevant and achievable.

Output Indicators – Output Indicators in Performance Measurement quantifies the services provided. They also help to determine resource allocation and areas where resources need to be increased or decreased dependant upon the workload of the service providers. For example, if it is found that goals are not being met and the service providers are carrying a heavy workload, then more resources should be allocated to that program if possible and vice versa. It is also important when assessing the cost of those services. Output indicators are useful when current accomplishments are compared to stated accomplishment goals. These indicators are necessary in determining whether or not programs are operating efficiently and according to goals. They are also an indicator as to whether a service offered is of value to citizens and promotes the overall good of the community.

Outcomes Indicators – Outcomes Indicators measure the results of services provided. For example, average scores of standardized tests may be used as an indicator of regarding the function of schools educational programs. By using Outcomes Indicators, federal agencies can evaluate the overall impact that the programs or services have on the community. Assessments using Outcomes Indicators allows for officials to discover and examine any deficiencies in the programs being assessed and to develop action plans as to how to overcome those deficiencies. These assessments also allow officials to compare previous results in order to assess the progress made toward specified goals. It is important to note that Outcome Indicators have many more facets than other indicators because the type of service provided may only be partially related to the outcomes and there may be other contributing factors to the Outcomes Indicator results.

Intermediate and end outcomes – An Intermediate Outcome is defined as an outcome that is expected to aid in the progression toward the end outcome, but is not the end outcome itself. The End Outcomes are often dependent upon the intermediate outcomes in order for stated goals to be realized. It is important to assess intermediate outcomes in order to ensure that the stated goals, or end outcomes are to be achieved. If it is found that through the assessment of intermediate outcomes that end outcomes are not likely to be realized, officials can develop a plan that will aid in the progression toward the stated goals or end outcomes. At that point, officials can also assess whether or not the program or service provided is operating efficiently and successfully delivering the goods and services it was designed to provide.

Efficiency measures – The most common Efficiency Measure in Performance Measurement is the Measurement of Unit Cost and is used to determine the level of efficiency at which a corporation or federal agency is operating. The Measurement of Unit Cost is found by measuring the inputs of a federal agency or corporation, against its' outcomes. Those outcomes are then compared to the stated goals and efficiency measures from prior years. Some important considerations must be made regarding the Efficiency Measures. It is important to take into account the quality of service and work provided. If the work or service provided is less costly, but lacks quality, the work may have to be redone. These types of instances affect the end result of Efficiency Measures resulting in skewed outcomes.

Input indicators -- Input Indicators measure the amount of resources used for providing a good or service. The results of Input Indicators can be reported as both financial and non-financial terms.

When financial information is used, the input information is often expressed in terms of cost in relation to the good or service and the dollar amount spent per capita. When non-financial information is used, the input information is often expressed in terms of capital assets and employee-days used to provide the good or service. By using both financial and non-financial measures, the federal agency or corporation can assess the accomplishments of its' goods or services being offered more completely by using the dollar costs, as well as the capital assets costs.

Selecting performance measures – In order for performance measurement reports to be relevant, the measures selected to assess performance should coincide with the corporation or federal agencies goals and objectives. In cases where it may be difficult to determine specific indicators for measuring performance, managers should begin with the stated goals and objectives and from there, determine what indicators best correlate with the functions and programs being evaluated. Finally, if the report is intended to be made available to the general public, managers should take care to include enough relevant measures and indicators to adequately explain performance. If too much information is given, this can lead to confusion by the user.

The limitation of the need for more than one indicator – The need for more than one indicator arises when a single performance measure does not adequately assess performance. This is apparent when comparing the performances of for-profit and not-for-profit corporations. The not-for-profit corporations' goal is to provide goods and services to better the lives of people or communities and the for-profit corporations are to increase shareholder wealth. A common indicator used in for-profit corporations is net profit as a measure of performance. This indicator cannot be used when measuring the services provided by non-for-profit corporations because making a profit is not one of the corporations primary objectives. In this case, other indicators should be developed for performance measurement.

The limitations in performance measurement when the cause and effect are not always evident – The relationship between the goals and objectives of a corporation or Federal Agency and its' performance is not always clear. While an activity may contribute to an end outcome, it may not always be the direct cause of the outcome. There may be many other contributing factors to the end results. For example, a school with a high dropout rate decides that it wants to decrease the dropout rate by hiring new teachers and increasing tutoring programs. This resulted in a lower dropout rate the following year. While hiring new teachers and increasing tutoring programs may have contributed to the end result, there may be other factors involved as well such as increased parental involvement or simply that a lesser number of students decided to drop out of high school than the year prior.

The limitation in performance measurement when performance indicators are in the formative stages – As advances are made in all fields, new performance measurements often need to be developed in order to adequately measure performance and outdated measures must be changed or removed completely because they no longer remain relevant. The problem that arises when performance measurements are still in the formative stages is that association between the measurement and the results may not yet be apparent because the performance measure is not yet fully developed. In regard to advances in areas such as technology or new services being offered, measuring the success of these advances may be difficult because there may not be a baseline or benchmark in which performance can be measured against.

Objectives and uses

OPM Work Force Model

The U.S. Office of Personnel Management's (OPM) Work Force Planning Model provides helpful guidelines for the implementation of any significant change in organizational processes. The main points are as follows:

- *Set strategic direction:* When attempting to manage and implement change managers should have an organized plan of objectives, conduct a comprehensive review of the overall organizational structure and set performance measures.
- *Supply, demand and discrepancies*: Managers should analyze the demographics of the permanent and temporary work forces and assess the skills of the organizations supervisors and department managers.

- *Implement and action plan:* A comprehensive plan regarding the reorganization process should be developed addressing stated goals and potential or existing deficiencies.
- *Implement action plan:* After development the plan should be implemented through effective communication, hiring new staff if necessary, adequate training and conducting reviews.
- *Monitor, evaluate and revise:* Once the plan is in place, it should be closely monitored for effectiveness. This gives the opportunity for managers to determine deficiencies in the reorganization plan and revise the plan as necessary.

Public accountability

Public accountability of Federal Agencies is becoming increasingly important. Currently, the Governmental Accounting Standards Board (GASB) provides a basic framework for reporting for public accountability.

- According to these standards, reports should be prepared in a manner that is understandable to its users, which should include the general public.
- All information should be reliable and relevant.
- The information should be all-inclusive as to the ways and means in which financial resources were obtained and used, the way in which the entity meets its financial obligations and the overall current and projected financial health of the federal agency.
- Basically, the GASB has stated that those funding federal agencies, i.e., taxpayers, have the right to know how those payments are being put to use and how future governmental debt burdens are going to affect them.

Performance reporting objectives

Performance reporting is used to as a means for corporations and federal agencies to report and discuss its' performance measurements with regulatory and/or legislative bodies and oversight committees. For corporations, Performance Reporting is used as a measure of corporate performance accountability to not only federal regulatory and oversight committees, but to its' shareholders and stakeholders as well. For federal agencies, Performance Reporting is used as a measure of accountability to federal regulatory and oversight committees as well as, the citizens that fund these federal agencies and programs through taxpayer dollars. The legislative branch of the federal government also utilizes federal agency and program Performance Reports in order to make decisions regarding the agency or program such as budgetary and resource acquisition decisions.

Accountability

In the public and private sectors, management, top executives and employees are expected to be held accountable for their performances. Without this accountability, corporations risk missing expected goals. For federal agencies and programs, the GASB determined that financial accountability and reports did not provide sufficient enough information for citizens, legislative bodies and oversight committees, to adequately gauge the success and failures of the federal agency or program. Therefore, in order to better gauge the successes of federal agencies and programs, the GPRA of 1993 was enacted in order to hold federal agencies responsible not only financially, but also for achieving its' goals and objectives. The inclusion of both financial and non-financial data in reports allows for legislative bodies and oversight committees as well as, the general public, to better assess the efficiency of a federal agency or program.

Managing for results

The concept of managing for results encompasses all levels of a corporate or government entity. Management must ensure that all guidelines regarding corporate and governmental goals, financial, budgetary and operational goals and purposes are clearly and thoroughly defined and communicated to all employees. GPRA standards require that performance reports be filed on yearly basis, within a five-year strategic plan structure. These performance reports must clearly define goals and objectives as well as, statements of performance goals that are measurable and plans as to how those goals are to be accomplished. Finally, if the stated goals have not been fully realized, the performance reports must include the level of progression toward those stated goals.

GPRA implementation guidance

The OMB helps federal agencies toward implementing GPRA guidelines as described in OMB Circular A-11, Part 6. This Circular gives an overview of specific definitions and defines the users of the Performance Plans and Reports. According to GPRA guidelines, these reports should be prepared with the following users in mind:

- *Agency officials and staff:* The report is used by agency officials and staff because they are the ones responsible for the overall operations of the program.
- *The president and Congress:* The president and Congress use the report in order for oversight as well as determining any changes in the programs and its' policies.
- *The public:* The reports are prepared in a way that is informative to the public as to the effectiveness of the program and the resources used for the program.

GPRA general goals

The GPRA defines general goals for strategic plans as those that describe the overall objectives of a federal agency and its' programs:

- The description of these goals should contain a sufficient amount of detail so the users of the strategic report plans can clearly determine the overall goals of the agency or program, without becoming overwhelmed.
- These goals should include the activities conducted toward the progression of stated goals over a period of time and provide the ways and means in which they will be evaluated in the future as to whether or not the goal was achieved.
- It is important to note that while the general goals describe the overall objectives of the agency or program, those stated goals should not be all encompassing to the point of being immeasurable or vague.

Performance, outcome, and output goals

The GPRA defines a *performance goal* as the desired level of performance of an agency or program in a fiscal year. This desired level of performance must possess the ability to be measured against actual performance. Performance goals should also be stated in a manner that is quantifiable and can be described as either outcome goals or output goals. Performance goals are largely based on stated general goals. The progressive achievement of performance goals is often used as a measure toward the achievement of general goals. In other words, the achievement of performance goals throughout the fiscal provides a basis for officials to adequately estimate whether or not general goals will be achieved. The GPRA defines outcome goals, as a description as to what the federal agency or program wants to achieve. Stated outcome goals should also refer to expected consequences of resulting from the activities of the federal agency or program. Output goals are defined as the expected activities to be performed over a specified period of time in order to achieve stated goals.

GPRA performance indicators definition

The GPRA defines performance Indicators as specific measures that are directly related to performance goals. Performance Indicators are used as a means to evaluate goal achievement and provide a basis for the measurable progression toward goal achievement throughout the year. Outcome measures as a performance indicator is described by the GPRA as a comparison of the results of the actions and programs offered by a federal agency and its' stated goals and objectives. Output measures used as a performance indicator are described by the GPRA as the actual documentation of the activities performed and efforts being made, toward the progression of achieving the federal agency or programs stated goals and objectives.

Elements and characteristics

Reliable data: Several activities help ensure that all information processed through the Financial Management System Data is reliable and accurate. Generally, the Information Technology department of a federal agency or organization maintains the overall financial management systems' hardware and software; however, the financial management department should maintain the reliability and accuracy over the financial data contained in the overall financial management system. The financial management department maintains control over the financial data and information by clearly defining the information inputs, defining the activities regarding how the information will be collected, how the information will be used and the prevention of performing the same activities more than once, achieves this. It is also important that the financial management department make sure that the financial information is readily available and accessible to authorized users and that all collected financial information is coordinated with other relevant information systems.

Calculating cost: When calculating costs for performance measures the Governmental Accounting Standards Board suggests that the accrual basis method of accounting is used and that both depreciation and indirect expenses are included. However, the GASB does not go into detail regarding what specific expenses are considered to be indirect. Until those specific definitions are provided, the GASB has stated that input costs at least include the following: Pension and other retiree benefit costs, other personnel fringe benefits and related judgments and claims of the good or service provided. These costs should be compared in a time-series of similarly defined costs. Comparing costs over time enables officials to determine the level of efficiency in which the program is operating and to make necessary changes when possible in order to increase program efficiency.

Explanatory information: Explanatory Information is included so that the users of the report can fully comprehend the information contained in the report and should also include quantitative and narrative information. This gives the users the ability to adequately assess performances. Explanatory Information also provides management the opportunity to give further details as to why actual performance did not meet expected performance goals. The quantitative information to be included in the report should encompass all the activities that are within the control of the federal agency or corporation. This includes economic, socio-economic, and environmental and decision making information. Narrative information is used to help explain issues such as why stated goals were not met, the importance of indicators used and budgetary shortfalls.

Baseline and benchmarking

Benchmarking is a generally a set of historic results in which the auditor can compare current audit results. Benchmarks are often established by the peer leaders of corporations and federal agencies by identifying and recording the best practices and processes of those peer leaders. Utilizing benchmarking processes allows for the federal agency or corporation to measure its collective progress toward achieving its' stated goals and objectives as well as achieving best practices in their respective industries.

Baselines are established through the process of gathering and measuring information. This is often conducting in order to establish the beginning of a trend. Baselines are also established and used when conducting project planning and evaluating project progress.

Economy, efficiency and effectiveness

The term *"economy"* used in performance measurement refers to the resources needed in order to accomplish the goals and objectives of the program or federal agency. This includes the determination of whether or not the proper amounts of resources have been acquired and if they have utilized accordingly. *Efficiency in performance measurement* refers to whether or not the resources acquired have been utilized in a manner that is most cost-effective. *Effectiveness in performance measurement* refers to the results of the program of federal agency and whether or not stated goals and objectives are being met. When using efficiency and economy as performance measurements, it is important that the data gathered in compared to a relevant benchmark. It is also important to note that all performance indicators be used when making decisions regarding programs.

Reporting legal requirements

The Government Performance and Results Act of 1993 (GPRA) state that governments must provide reports that include statements of goals, the processes developed in order to achieve stated goals and a comparison to stated and actual goals. The Government Management Reform Act 1994 (GMRA) states that federal agencies must submit an audited financial statement from the previous fiscal year to the Office of Management and Budgets. It must include performance outputs and outcomes. They must also include a statement that clearly defines its' goals, its' year-to-date accomplishments and the financial results relevant to those accomplishments. If the stated goals are not being met, federal agencies must submit the reasons they have not been met and what, if any, improvements can be made toward the accomplishment of stated and expected goals.

Sources of performance data

One of the major sources of performance information is the record of daily business activities and transactions. This information often comes from the lower levels of operation for the federal agency or program. This information is necessary in order to report on resources used, the success of the program or agency and for budgetary planning. For some federal agencies and program, performance information may be gathered through physical testing. *An example of a federal agency that utilizes physical testing is the Department of Environmental Quality (DEQ).* The DEQ performs physical tests in order to determine the air and water quality of its' respective area. Another source of performance data is to conduct citizen surveys. This involves asking relevant questions through mailed surveys or personal interviews of area citizens. Gathering Economic and Demographic information from sources such as the Federal Bureau of the Census will help officials assess its' achievements or determine a further need for its' economic development programs. Finally, all financial information and reports are a main source of Performance Information.

GPRA of 1993

The Government Performance Reporting Act (GPRA) of 1993 created legislation that required the management of corporations and Federal Agencies to develop an integrated management system that included 5 year strategic plans, annual performance plans and program performance reports. The GPRA was enacted:

- To aid in decision-making
- To promote accountability in performance for corporations and Federal Agencies
- To improve public perception and confidence
- To improve efficiency in government programs
- Improve service quality and customer satisfaction
- To improve internal management

Finally, performance reports of Federal Agencies that are made public are required to include clearly stated goals and objectives and the achievement or progression toward those goals.

Guidelines for strategic plans

The GPRA requires federal agencies to develop a strategic plan of at least five years. These five-year plans must be updated every three years and the agency must consult with Congress while developing their strategic plans. The plans are required to include the following:

- *Mission statement:* The mission statement must clearly describe the main goals, functions and operations of the agency.
- *General goals:* The agency must also state its' general goals and objectives.
- *Goal achievement:* The agency must describe the planned activities and resources required toward the achievement of stated goals and objectives.
- *Relationship of performance goals to general goals:* This relationship should be described in the strategic plan.
- *External factors:* The agency must include a description of external factors that may affect the agencies goal achievement.
- *Program evaluations:* Strategic plans must include the evaluation activities and techniques that are to be used when determining goals. Evaluation activities used for revising previously stated goals should also be described.

Guidelines for performance plans

Performance plans are to be completed on a yearly basis and should include the following components:

- *Established performance goals:* Federal agencies must identify the goals to be achieved over the course of the year. The established goals must be measurable in order to determine successes and failures.
- *Description of strategies:* Federal agencies must give a brief account of the planned activities and required capital assets in order to achieve of established goals.
- *Comparative:* Federal agencies must describe the ways and means in which stated goals are compared with actual performance.
- Finally, the federal agencies must establish the activities it plans to use for substantiating and validating performance measurements.

In a case where quantifiable goals cannot be established, federal agencies should consult with the OMB in order to determine the proper form of identifying goals.

Performance reports elements

Performance reports must be filed on a yearly basis for the purpose of reviewing the agencies performance toward goal achievement. These reports should include the goals that were achieved, the progression toward goals that were not yet achieved at the time of performance report filing, the goals that were not achieved and the reasons behind why they were not achieved. All annual reports must also include the goals achieved for the three previous years. Audited financial statements must also be filed with performance reports. Performance Reports must also include the following components:

- *Reviews:* The report must contain a review of all goals achieved.
- *Evaluation:* The report must contain an evaluation that compares the actual goals achieved to the planned goals.
- *Explanation:* An explanation of all goals not achieved and an established plan as to how the agency plans on meeting those goals in the future.
- *Summary:* A summary of evaluations completed for a program and the measures used in program evaluation. The summary should also include whether or not planned goals and objectives were achieved.

Annual performance plans

The OMB has provided additional factors and guidelines for developing and reporting on performance plans and are as follows:

- The performance plans' focus should be on the program of agencies main goals and objectives.
- Performance plans and reports should clearly state the programs main goals and objectives.
- Performance plans and reports should be prepared in a manner that is objective and all measures used should be quantifiable.
- Supporting evidence should be given regarding support of outcomes.

- Performance plans and reports should describe the main characteristics of the program or federal agency.
- Finally, a recent OMB requirement dictates that performance plans and performance based budget plans be submitted simultaneously due to the fact that the two are interrelated.

Annual program performance reports

The OMB has provided the following additional guidelines regarding Annual Program Performance Reports:

- Annual performance reports must provide a comparison of stated and actual goals.
- The report must also contain an explanation regarding the progression toward stated goals that were not yet achieved at the time of report filing.
- The report must contain the planned activities in order to achieve goals and objectives that have not yet been met.
- All performance reports are to cover a total of four fiscal years, the current fiscal year and the three previous.
- The report must include all performance goals stated in the annual performance plan.
- The report may also include general goals if it is considered to be both a general goal and performance goal.
- The OMB does not dictate a particular format in which the annual program performance reports must be filed.

Financial and nonfinancial performance measures

As part of performance measures, it is important to review both financial and nonfinancial data. Financial measures are objective and include annual earnings, return on assets, cost reductions, adjustments, bad debt write-offs, inventory counts, and budget adherence. All of these items work together to form a picture of how an organization (or a department within an organization) is performing. However, financial measures alone often do not tell the entire story. As a result, nonfinancial data often needs to be reviewed. This includes things like customer satisfaction, employee satisfaction, and quality of work performed. While these are hard to quantify as they can be subjective measures, they help to tell the entire story about overall performance.

Financial and Managerial Analysis Techniques

Time-value of money

The time-value of money concept is simply evaluating the purchase power of a dollar over time. Corporations utilize the time-value of money concept in order to ensure that there will be sufficient operating funds in the future if major capital expenditures occur in the present. When making major capital expenditure decisions, corporate executives want to make sure, to the extent possible, that a reasonable return or profit will be realized from such expenditures. Another situation where the time-value of money concept is considered is when corporate executives are evaluating the immediate expenses and returns against the long-term expenses and returns of a major capital expenditure.

Cash-flow analysis

When conducting financial analysis, it is important that managers determine the amount of cash coming in to the corporation, as well as the amount of cash paid out by the corporation. This can be done by analyzing accounts payable and accounts receivable.

When considering new major capital expenditures such as purchasing new buildings and/or equipment, launching new product lines or implementing new programs, the cost of these expenditures should be measured against the potential revenue generated in order to reach a reasonable conclusion of cash flows. It is important to note that when conducting a cash-flow analysis, non-government corporations must take into consideration taxes before using any Time-Value of Money techniques. Most government agencies are not subject to taxes and consequently do not have to take them into consideration when evaluating major capital expenditures.

Future value analyses

Future value analysis involves the expected value of an investment over a period of time. This is achieved by taking the dollar amount invested and the expected rate of interest earned and calculating the expected return over a given period of time. There are many factors that affect Future Value calculations. When making these decisions, management should also consider whether or not the interest is compounded, meaning that the interest earned on the investment is re-invested as principal and therefore earns interest as well. Also, historical interest rates should be taken into considerations in order to determine whether or not it fluctuates radically over time. Evaluating the past history of 5 years or more of an investment will allow managers to adequately evaluate expected future performance.

Present value analyses

Net present value analysis is used when determining the amount of funds needed today, or in the present, to earn a specified amount by a future date. When calculating the net present value of an investment, managers must take into consideration total value necessary, the interest rate and amount of time being considered. When the determinations of interest rate and future value have been made, managers can then find the net present value by discounting the investments' future value. The discount rate used in this process is the given interest rate of the investment. Calculating present values is often used when planning for known future major expenditures such as early retirement packages, employee severance packages or changes in laws in regulations that will require the corporation to make major expenditures updating equipment or information systems.

Flowcharting

Flowcharts allow for visual and graphic representations of a process that is being reviewed that involves many steps:
- These graphic representations of often-complicated processes helps the personnel involved understand and review relevant information.
- These flow charts ensure that all relevant personnel are "on the same page" and help to prevent miscommunication and misunderstandings. Once everyone has a full

understanding of the processes, the information can be adequately analyzed and key decisions can be made.

- Flowcharting is also a useful tool when making decisions regarding the ranking of issues of importance.

- Issues that are found to be less significant can be removed in order to concentrate on what are determined to be more important issues.

Regression analysis

Regression analysis allows for management to determine and define the relationship between variables. The variables used in regression analysis are often referred to as constant or non-random and dependent or random. The main importance of using regression analysis is that it determines whether or not variables are dependent upon one another and also, the level at which the variables are dependent. A simple example of regression analysis is if a corporation is trying to determine how many sales people they need to hire. The number of sales people hired is dependent upon the amount of inventory available. Any additional amount of inventory needed is dependent upon the amount of inventory sold by the new sales people.

The main result categories of regression analysis results:
- *Direct relationship:* When both the independent and dependent variables increase. Using the sales person example, it means that as new sales people hires increase, so does the requests for additional inventory.

- *Inverse relationship:* When the independent variable increases, but the dependent variable decreases. Continuing to use the same example, this means that as new sales people hires increase, the amount of requested additional inventory decreases.

- *Non-linear relationship:* This relationship occurs when the independent or non-random variable is found to have no impact on the dependant or random variable. Using the same examples from above, this means that the new sales people hires have had no impact on requests for additional inventory.

<u>The limits pertaining to regression analysis:</u>

- Care should be taken to ensure that all data inputs used in regression analysis are accurate and reliable.
- If the information is not accurate or reliable, then it renders the regression analysis ineffectual.
- If there is found that the variables have an insignificant relationship to one another, then the Regression Analysis is also ineffective and unreliable.
- Also, all information gathered and data inputs should be within a workable and relevant range.
- Finally, it is important to understand that the relationship found during regression analysis does not necessarily mean that one variable is the cause or determining factor of another variable.

Financial condition analysis

Financial condition analysis is used to provide a larger scope of the overall short-term and long-term financial health of a corporation. This assessment is necessary when determining long and short-term capital expenditures, long and short term budget forecasting and helping to detect any indication of existing or possible future financial distress. In financial condition analysis, financial managers may isolate particular ratios that are most useful to the task they are performing. Finally, financial condition analysis also takes into consideration non-financial factors that contribute to the overall financial health of a corporation such as those that are administrative or economic.

Financial statement ratio analysis

Financial statement ratio analysis is an important tool in managing day-to-day financial management activities. This is not only important for determining cash in-flows and out-flows, but impacts many areas as well. This analysis is also utilized as a comparison against industry norms. Financial statement ratio analysis helps to determine whether or not internal controls over financial management are adequate and operating properly, that all policies and procedures are being followed and if the terms of various contract agreements are being met. Finally, a financial statement ratio analysis is needed when performing long-term budgeting and forecasting.

The techniques regarding the conversion of data to ratios for the financial statement ratio analysis – The raw data from financial statements may be difficult to understand for those not directly involved in the process. The data must then, be converted into forms that are more useful and user friendly. One way to convert this data is to use common size statements. Common size statements offer the analyst or the user the ability to quickly determine whether or not assets are disproportionate to liabilities, payables are disproportionate to receivables or if expenditures are disproportionately high. Another useful process of converting financial data is by Per Capita Information. This process follows the financial information over a period of time and compares the results to the results of other corporations within its industry.

Time-series analysis

Conducting a time-series analysis allows for financial analysts to determine the performance of a particular financial statement over a period of time. This also allows for analysts to further investigate any problems or inconsistencies found and to come to a solution in order to prevent any additional negative financial consequences in the future. It is important to note that if inconsistencies or problems are detected, that further investigation must be done in order to determine why they occurred or what caused them to occur. Conducting a time-series analysis gives the financial analysis a starting point or basis for such investigations.

Comparative analysis

A comparative analysis of financial statement ratios is conducted by comparing the corporations' ratios with the ratios of a similar corporation within its industry or against an industry benchmark. Industry benchmarks are often provided by credit rating agencies. If it is found that there are no industry benchmarks, then financial analysts should be sure to compare their ratios with a corporation that is of similar size and offer similar services. As with Time-Series analysis, comparative analysis offers financial analysts a means by which they can detect and problems or inconsistencies and to provide a starting point of investigation into why they occurred or what caused them to occur.

Key liquidity ratios

Liquidity ratios are used to help determine whether or not a corporation or federal agency is currently able to meet its' short tem financial obligations. The most common liquidity ratios used are current ratios and quick ratios.

- The current ratio measures current assets against current liabilities. Current assets for this ratio are assets that are expected to be used within one year. Current assets for this ratio are cash, cash equivalents and short-term investments that are easily converted into cash.
- The quick ratios measures cash, cash equivalents and short-term investments over current liabilities. Current assets that are highly liquid or easily convertible are not used in the Quick Ratio equation.

Key Asset Turnover Efficiency Ratios

Asset turnover ratios are used to determine how quickly a corporation coverts assets or inventory into cash. The most common ratios for measuring asset turnover efficiency are:

- *Average days in receivables:* Measures ending receivables against revenues divided by 365 (the number of days in a year).
- *Inventory turnover*: Found by dividing the cost of goods sold by the average inventor.
- *Total asset turnover:* Measured by dividing total revenues by total assets.

Using these ratios helps corporations to discover various problems in internal controls such as controls over Inventory and Supplies as well as controls over credit management and debt collection.

Budget solvency and operating results

Budget solvency and operating results ratios are used to determine whether or not the corporation generates enough income in order to meet its debt obligations or expenses. This also allows for financial analysts to discover any financial weaknesses and develop plans as to how to correct those weaknesses. These ratios are also important for governments or corporations that borrow in long-term debt instruments or markets that require fixed payments. Using budget solvency ratios allow for budget planners and forecasters to set aside funds for the purpose of unforeseen events that may directly affect the corporation such as severe economic downturns and other events that are beyond the corporations' control.

Earnings margin ratio

The earnings margin ratio is found by dividing the change in net assets by the operating revenues. This ratio gives financial analysts a rough estimate of net profits in a corporation. Analysts use this ratio in order to determine profitability and whether or not the corporation can meet its' financial obligations. Earnings margin ratios should be measured in a time series such as year-over-year. Measuring earnings margin ratio over a period of time gives the analysts a clearer picture regarding the financial health of a corporation. Any profits realized from a non-recurring business transition, such as the sale of a subsidiary, should be considered separately from the earnings margin ratio calculation. Analysts also use this ratio to determine the cause and effect of budget deficits and surpluses.

Budgetary cushion

Budgetary cushion is determined by dividing the total unreserved fund balance by the total revenues and transfers in. For state and local governments, the results of this ratio are used by credit agencies to determine credit quality. Credit ratings are used by investors in order determine the likelihood of credit default. The amount of funds set aside as a budgetary cushion for corporations is generally dependent upon the cost of its' business operations. The budgetary cushion should be adequate enough to cover negative economic events as well as operating expenses. The amount of budgetary cushions in governments based on credit rating agencies is 5-10 percent of annual revenues. Also, governments are expected to have a budgetary cushion that covers what are considered regular expenses and do not necessarily need to take possible negative economics events into consideration.

Long-term financial flexibility ratios

Long-term financial flexibility ratios are used to determine and measure:
A corporations' current outstanding debt
Its ability to pay back that debt
Whether or not the corporation will be able to continue to meet its obligations if additional capital funding is acquired through debt financing.
By calculating these ratios, the corporation is able to determine how much capital is needed to pay back debt obligations and how much capital can be dedicated to other corporate endeavors. Long-Term flexibility ratios are necessary for assessing the corporations' debt management and are also a useful tool when assessing the internal controls over the financial management of long-term debt.

Debt burden

The debt burden ratio is calculated by dividing the outstanding long-term debt by population. For both governments and corporations, this calculation is used specifically to determine whether or not the entity has the ability to pay off long-term debt. For corporations, the outstanding long-term debt may be divided by income and for governments; the outstanding long-term debt may be divided by revenues generated from such things as property taxes and state and local taxes. It is important to note that governments can get a clearer picture of its debt burden by taking into consideration per capita debt and the income of the community's residents. Governments and corporations that have a low debt-burden are considered to be more financially flexible when it comes to acquiring additional capital funding through long-term debt.

Debt service burden

The debt service burden is calculated by dividing total debt service by total revenues. For both governments and corporations, calculating the debt service burden allows for financial managers to determine the dollar amount that is dedicated to paying off long-term debt and therefore, is not available for other business or daily operating activities.

When calculating the debt service burden, financial managers should also take into consideration the amortization schedule of the debt principal. If a government or corporate debt service burden is found to be a high percentage, the entity is considered to be less financially flexible when it comes to acquiring additional capital funding through long-term debt.

Debt service coverage

The debt service Coverage ratio is calculated by dividing excess of revenues over expenses plus, depreciation and interest expenses by principal payment plus interest expense. The basic principal of debt service coverage is to determine whether or not a government or corporation has the ability to finance the debt of what their respective business activities. Debt service coverage ratios determine whether the corporation or government is generating enough income or revenues in order to pay debt obligations. If the income just barely covers the debt, then there are no funds available for any other business or operating activities. In this case, the debt burden is too high. If the debt burden is too high, then both governments and corporations risk not only the inability to pay off existing debt, but also a low credit rating by credit rating agencies indicating that the entity has a high level of credit default.

Pension funded ratio

Pension funded ratios are calculated by dividing pension fund assets by pension benefit obligation. This calculation may be more geared toward governments as fewer and fewer corporations continue to offer pension funds, instead opting for 401k and IRA plans. The amount of funds needed for pensions is considered a long-term debt obligation because of the financing needs of future pension fund payments, but current pension fund payments or liabilities must also be taken into consideration as well. If the current earnings on assets do not cover the amount needed to fund the pension program, the pension is said to be under funded. If this trend continues, then the government or corporation will not be able to meet its' future pension obligations.

Pay-back analysis

The payback analysis determines the length of time in which the initial invested amount will be recovered and the investment will begin to earn money. This is also referred to as a break even point. Payback analyses are often used in conjunction with other financial measures. The importance of using payback analysis is not only to estimate the turn-around time from the initial capital investment layout to when that layout is paid back and the investment begins to earn new capital, but also as a risk assessment tool. If an investment has a shorter payback period, then the investment is considered less risky than those that have a longer payback period. Payback analysis is widely because of it is considered one of the more simple and easy to use financial measures.

Practice Test

Practice Questions

1. Which internal control component is used to assess the quality of internal control performance?
   a. Control Environment
   b. Risk Assessment
   c. Information and Communication
   d. Monitoring

2. What role does the Chief Executive Officer play in an organization's internal control system?
   a. Designing and implementing effective internal control
   b. Providing governance, guidance and oversight of the internal control system
   c. Measuring the effectiveness of internal controls
   d. Establishing internal control policies and procedures

3. What role do internal controls play in risk management?
   a. Eliminate risk
   b. Create risk management procedures
   c. Identify risks and ensure actions are taken to reduce risks
   d. Prioritize risks based on threat level

4. Which internal control activity attempts to reduce fraud and errors by separating tasks between job functions?
   a. Controls over information processing
   b. Authorization of transactions
   c. Physical safeguards
   d. Segregation of duties

5. A positive control environment affects the quality of internal control by...
   a. providing discipline and structure
   b. implementing goals and procedures
   c. eliminating fraud, waste and misuse
   d. establishing an information technology system to implement internal control procedures

6. An individual auditor assigned to an audit project would not necessarily be required to possess which of the following sets of knowledge?
   a. Professional knowledge and competence in auditing
   b. Knowledge of the operations of the federal agency being audited
   c. Knowledge of the fieldwork standards for various audits
   d. Knowledge of information processing systems and information technology control measures

7. According to the financial management and control principles of the Government Accountability Office, internal controls are used to meet a corporation's overall objectives by...
    a. providing a cost/benefit analysis of the objectives
    b. creating an ethical environment
    c. acting as a system of checks and balances
    d. developing control procedures and systems

8. What is the continuing professional education requirement for auditors acting under the rules and guidelines of the government auditing standards?
    a. 80 hours of continuing professional education every two years
    b. 60 hours of continuing professional education every two years
    c. 90 hours of continuing professional education every three years
    d. 80 hours of continuing professional education every three years

9. According to the Government Accountability Office Yellow Book, which three classes of impairment may affect an auditor's objective judgment?
    a. Personal, conflict of interest and organizational
    b. Personal, external and organizational
    c. Conflict of interest, external and organizational
    d. Personal, external and conflict of interest

10. Non-federal agencies with expenditures under _____ are exempt from an audit by a federal audit agency.
    a. $500,000
    b. $250,000
    c. $300,000
    d. $650,000

11. In performance measurement, what are expected goals measured against to determine an organization's progress toward achieving its goals?
    a. Financial statement ratios
    b. Income statement amount
    c. Actual performance
    d. Internal control procedures

12. What is the most common efficiency measure in performance measurement?
    a. Unit cost
    b. Unit sales price
    c. Unit production quantity
    d. Unit quality

13. For federal agencies, which term refers to the resources needed to accomplish the goals and objectives of their programs?
    a. Efficiency
    b. Effectiveness
    c. Economy
    d. Efficacy

14. What is the major source of performance information for a federal agency or program?
    a. Public use surveys
    b. Financial reports
    c. Demographic information
    d. Daily business activities and transactions

15. According to Government Performance And Results Act guidelines, which of the following components is not included in a performance plan?
    a. Established performance goals
    b. Description of strategies
    c. Comparative
    d. Goals and directives

16. Which financial analysis method takes in the expected value of an investment over a period of time?
    a. Cash Flow method
    b. Future Value Analysis
    c. Present Value Analysis
    d. Rate of Return

17. Which analysis method determines the performance of a financial statement over a period of time?
    a. Regression Analysis
    b. Financial Condition Analysis
    c. Time Series Analysis
    d. Financial Statement Ratio Analysis

18. Which analysis method can financial analysts use to detect inconsistencies in financial statements?
    a. Regression Analysis
    b. Time Series Analysis
    c. Financial Condition Analysis
    d. Comparative Analysis

19. Which of the following ratios help an agency detect problems in internal controls?
    a. Asset turnover ratio
    b. Liquidity ratio
    c. Earnings margin ratio
    d. Efficiency ratio

20. The purpose of Payback Analysis is to determine...
    a. how well an agency can pay its expenses
    b. when monies invested will be recovered
    c. the rate of return on an investment
    d. how well an agency can pay long-term debt

21. How are pension funded ratios calculated?
    a. Pension fund assets divided by pension benefit obligation
    b. Pension fund assets divided by pension beneficiaries
    c. Pension benefit obligation divided by pension fund assets
    d. Pension benefit obligation divided by pension beneficiaries

22. What does the Debt Burden Ratio calculate?
    a. The ratio of debt of assets
    b. The ability of an entity to make short-term loan payments
    c. The ability of an entity to pay off long-term debt
    d. The ability of an entity to incur debt to finance a capital asset purchase

23. Which financial measure is used by investors to determine the likelihood of a credit default?
    a. Long-term financial flexibility ratios
    b. Key budget solvency
    c. Budgetary cushion
    d. Earnings margin ratio

24. What is the purpose of benchmarking?
    a. To establish the beginning of a trend
    b. To measure performance accountability
    c. To compare current audit results with historic results
    d. To hold government financial managers accountable for performance

25. Why is it important that financial management systems be monitored on a regular and ongoing basis?
    a. To test the information technology controls
    b. To determine if systems are meeting requirements and objectives
    c. To check the system for errors and fraud
    d. To assess the need for changes to the system

Answer Key and Explanations

1. D: Monitoring. Internal control helps to ensure that an organization's objectives have been achieved. The objectives covered by internal control are effectiveness and efficiency of operations, reliability of financial reports and compliance with regulations and laws. The five components of internal control are:

- The Control Environment— the foundation of the internal control process that provides an organization's employees a basis to affect internal control processes
- Risk Assessment— the identification, management and analysis of risks that may affect the performance of an organization
- Information and Communication—systems that identify, collect, and distribute information for employees to perform their duties
- Control Activities— processes that ensure management's directions are followed
- Monitoring— process used to determine the quality of internal control performance

2. A: Designing and implementing effective internal control. The Chief Executive Officer is responsible for designing and implementing effective internal controls, providing direction and leadership to senior management and ensuring that senior management is fostering an effective internal control environment. The internal control process involves employees at every level. Senior management is tasked with establishing internal control policies and procedures, and ensuring that each organizational unit is implementing internal control procedures effectively. Internal and external auditors measure the effectiveness of internal control, assess the design and implementation of internal controls, and recommend ways in which the internal control system may be improved. The Board of Directors provides governance, guidance and oversight of the internal control system.

3. C: Identify risks and ensure actions are taken to reduce risks. Risk management is the identification, assessment and prioritization of risks. The objectives of risk management are to minimize, monitor and control the instances and effects of unfortunate events. Internal controls are used in the risk management process to make certain that risks are identified, and that actions are taken to reduce the consequences of an unfortunate event. Internal controls are designed to respond to the occurrence of a risk and to provide a risk treatment.

4. D: Segregation of duties. Internal controls are categorized by either the objective or the nature of the control. There are several types of activity internal controls:

- Segregation of duties reduces fraud or error by one person by assigning the authorization, custody, and record keeping roles to several people
- Authorization of transactions is the review of transactions by an appropriate person
- Retention of records requires documentation be maintained to validate transactions
- Supervision or monitoring of operations provides oversight of operational activity
- Physical safeguards are the use of cameras, locks, and other devices to protect assets.
- Top level reviews provide an analysis of actual results versus organizational goals or plans
- IT Security ensures that security tools such as passwords and access logs limit access to data

- Controls over information processing include edit checks, accounting for transactions in numerical sequences, reconciliation of accounts, and access control

5. A: Providing discipline and structure. Management and employees are responsible for establishing and maintaining an environment that nurtures a positive, supportive attitude toward internal control. The positive support provides the benefits of discipline and structure, and fosters a work culture that augments the quality of internal control. Agency management plays a key role in providing leadership in setting and maintaining the organization's ethical tone, providing guidance for proper behavior, removing temptations for unethical behavior and implementing discipline when appropriate.

6. D: Knowledge of information processing systems and information technology control measures. When an auditing agency assigns auditors, the agency needs to ensure that the auditors:
- Possess adequate professional knowledge and competence in applicable auditing standards such as GAGAS, GAO and AICPA standards
- Obtain overall and general knowledge regarding the operations of the federal agency or corporation being audited
- Possess adequate communication skills in addition to the skills necessary to complete all audit tasks
- Possess adequate knowledge regarding the fieldwork standards for various audits
- Know GAAP

An individual auditor may not be required to possess all of the skills described above, however, the auditing agency staff should possess these skills as a collective whole.

7. C: Acting as a system of checks and balances. A system of checks and balances is achieved by a management team's adherence to the Government Accountability Office financial management and control principles. These include:
- Adherence to laws, rules and regulations as they specifically apply to the corporation
- Assurance that all financial reporting, including budgets, earnings forecasts and financial statements (whether for internal or external use), are trustworthy, truthful and reliable
- Corporate resources are used in a manner that is effective, efficient and ethical

While implementing an internal controls system, management should perform a cost/benefit analysis and critically evaluate outside factors that may determine the efficiency of such controls. Finally, although internal controls may help instill confidence in the attainment of corporate goals, they are not a guarantee that those goals will be met.

8. A: 80 hours of continuing professional education every two years. Auditors acting under the rules and guidelines of the government auditing standards are required to complete a minimum of 80 hours of continuing professional education every two years. The purpose of this continuing education is to gain increased knowledge and proficiency in the auditor's work. The Government Accountability Office notes that its particular continuing professional education requirements may differ from requirements of other agencies such as state licensing boards and professional organizations.

9. B: Personal, external and organizational. Auditors and auditing agencies must maintain a level of autonomy in order to reach objective and impartial conclusions and recommendations. The three classes defined by the Government Accountability Office Yellow Book that may impair an auditor's objective judgment are personal, external and organizational.

- Personal impairments can include personal relationships or beliefs that may affect an auditor's judgment, therefore preventing the auditor from performing the duties objectively and impartially
- External impairments can occur when the auditor is experiencing pressure, either actual or perceived, by corporate executives and/or employees
- Organizational impairments can occur when the auditor's judgment is affected due to the individual auditor's and/or the auditing agency's position within the government

10. C: $300,000. Single audits or program-specific audits must be conducted for all non-federal agencies that spend $300,000 or more in federal award monies during a fiscal year. Non-federal agencies that spend less than $300,000 in federally-awarded monies are exempt from these auditing requirements. The Office of Management and Budget (OMB), in Circular A-133, provides guidelines for federal audit agencies that conduct audits of non-federal agencies receiving federal awards and grants. It also states that a program-specific audit may be conducted if the federal award money pertains to only one major program. The general scope of this type of audit regarding financial statements, internal controls, compliance and follow-up are the same as when performing audits for entities that don't receive government funds. Additional requirements for reporting include submitting the audit information collected, in proper form, to a federal clearinghouse designated by the OMB.

11. C: Actual performance. Performance measurements evaluate whether or not a federal agency is achieving its stated or expected goals. Expected goals are measured against actual performance to determine the agency's progress. Before a performance measurement evaluation begins, a plan is defined, and specific areas of performance evaluation are determined. This helps to ensure that relevant areas are being reviewed, and that time and resources are not wasted in measuring irrelevant subjects. Typical subjects for performance measurement review include financial data, public perception, overall business activities and employee performance and satisfaction levels.

12. A: Unit cost. The most common efficiency measure in performance measurement is unit cost. Measurement consists of comparing the inputs of a federal agency against its outcomes, then comparing the outcomes to the stated goals and efficiency measures from prior years. This measure helps determine the level of efficiency at which a federal agency operates. Some important considerations, such as quality of service and scope of work provided, must be made regarding efficiency measures, since less costly but low quality work may have to be redone, therefore impacting efficiency.

13. C: Economy. In performance measurement, economy refers to the resources needed in order to accomplish the goals and objectives of the program or federal agency. This measurement checks if proper amounts of resources have been acquired, and if they've been utilized accordingly. Efficiency determines whether or not the resources acquired have been utilized in a manner that is

most cost-effective. Effectiveness refers to the result of the program or federal agency, and whether or not stated goals and objectives are being met.

14. D: Daily business activities and transactions. The major source of performance information is the record of daily business activities and transactions. This information is necessary to track resources used and the success of the program or agency. It is also critical to budgetary planning. Another source of performance data is to conduct local citizen surveys; by mail or in-person interviews. Gathering economic and demographic information from sources such as the Federal Bureau of the Census can also help an agency's officials assess achievements or determine a further need for its economic development programs. Finally, financial information and reports are a source of performance information.

15. D: Goals and directives. The Government Performance And Results Act requires performance plans to be completed annually. The inclusion of goals and directives is not required, but the plans should include the following components:
- Established performance goals— federal agencies must identify the goals to be achieved over the course of the year. The established goals must be measurable in order to determine successes and failures
- Description of Strategies— federal agencies must give a brief account of the planned activities and required capital assets in order to achieve established goals
- Comparative— federal agencies must describe the ways and means in which stated goals are compared with actual performance

16. B: Future value analysis. Future value analysis is used to determine the expected value of an investment over a period of time. When considering new major capital expenditures, such as purchasing new buildings and/or equipment, launching new product lines or implementing new programs, the cost of these expenditures should be measured against the potential revenue generated in order to reach a reasonable conclusion of cash flows. Future value is calculated using the dollar amount invested, the expected rate of interest, and a time variable. Present value analysis is used when determining the amount of funds needed today, or in the present, to earn a specified amount by a future date. When calculating the present value of an investment, managers must take into consideration total value necessary, the interest rate and amount of time being considered.

17. C: Time Series Analysis. Time Series Analysis uses an ordered sequence of values of a variable at equally-spaced intervals. It determines the performance of a particular financial statement over a period of time. Financial Statement Ratio Analysis is an important tool in managing day-to-day financial management activities. It determines cash in-flows and out-flows, is utilized as a comparison against industry norms, and determines whether or not internal controls over financial management are adequate and operating properly. Financial Condition Analysis is used to provide a larger scope of the overall short-term and long-term financial health of a corporation. Regression Analysis allows for management to determine and define the relationship between variables for the purpose of determining future value.

18. B: Time Series Analysis. Conducting a Time Series Analysis allows analysts to investigate problems and inconsistencies, and to form a solution that would prevent additional negative

financial consequences in the future. It is important to note that if inconsistencies or problems are detected, further investigation must be done to determine why they occurred, or pinpoint the causative factors. Used this way, Time Series Analysis determines the starting point, or basis, for such investigations.

19. A: Asset turnover ratio. Asset turnover ratios determine how quickly a corporation monetizes assets or inventory. The most common ratios for measuring Asset Turnover efficiency are:
- Average Days in Receivables— measures ending receivables against revenues, divided by 365 (the number of days in a year).
- Inventory Turnover— found by dividing the cost of goods sold by the average inventory
- Total Asset Turnover— measured by dividing total revenues by total assets

Using these ratios would also help uncover or discover various problems in internal controls, such as controls over inventory and supplies, credit management and debt collection.

20. B: When monies invested will be recovered. Payback Analysis determines the length of time in which an invested amount will be recovered and begin to earn money— the breakeven point. This is considered the point at which a business, project or product is "financially viable." Understandably, Payback Analysis proves to be a reliable risk assessment tool. If the payback analysis yields an investment with a shorter payback period, then that investment would be considered less risky than one with a longer payback period. Payback analysis is widely used because it's considered one of the simpler financial measures, and it's often used in conjunction with other financial measures.

21. A: Pension fund assets divided by pension benefit obligation. Pension Funded Ratios are calculated by dividing pension fund assets by pension benefit obligation. This calculation may be more geared toward governments, as corporations continue to move away from defined benefit plans toward defined contribution plans, such as a 401(k). Money needed for pensions is considered a long-term debt obligation because of the financing needs of future pension fund payments, but current pension fund payments or liabilities must also be taken into consideration. If the current earnings on assets do not cover the amount needed to fund the pension program, the pension is said to be under-funded. If this trend continues, then the entity would not be able to meet its future pension obligations.

22. C: The ability of an entity to pay off long-term debt. Debt burden is the cost of servicing debt. The ratio is used to determine an entity's ability to pay off long-term debt. In the case of government, the debt burden is the cost of the outstanding long-term debt divided by its revenues, which are generated from taxes. A government can get a clearer picture of its debt burden by taking into consideration per capita debt and the income of the community's residents. A low debt-burden places the entity in a more financially advantageous position, particularly if trying to float more long-term debt.

23. C: Budgetary cushion. Budgetary cushion is determined by dividing the total unreserved fund balance by the total revenues and transfers in. For state and local governments, the results of this ratio are one of the factors used by credit agencies to assign credit ratings, which are, in turn, used by potential investors to determine the likelihood of credit default. The amount of funds set aside as

a budgetary cushion for corporations is generally dependent on the cost of its business operations, but it's generally adequate to cover negative economic events as well as operating expenses. The amount of budgetary cushions in governments, based on credit rating agencies, is 5-10% of annual revenues. Governments are expected to have a budgetary cushion that covers regular expenses, but do not necessarily need to allow for possible negative economic events.

24. C: To compare current audit results with historic results. Benchmarking is generally a set of historic results to which an auditor can compare current audit results. Benchmarks are often established by identifying and recording the best practices and processes of leaders of peer corporations or federal agencies. Utilizing benchmarking processes allow an agency or corporation to measure its progress toward achieving stated goals and objectives, as well as best practices.

25. B: To determine if systems are meeting requirements and objectives. The regular and ongoing monitoring of financial management systems is necessary to assess the systems' effectiveness in meeting requirements and objectives. Additionally, ongoing monitoring helps assure that systems operate in the manner for which they were designed. When new systems are implemented, an evaluation should compare the previous financial system processes with current system processes to determine whether or not the desired goals of the new system have been achieved. Officials should also test to learn if users have successfully accepted and implemented the new financial management systems. All data gathered during the evaluation of financial management systems should be quantified in order to adequately measure the levels of success and failure.

Secret Key #1 - Time is Your Greatest Enemy

Pace Yourself

Wear a watch. At the beginning of the test, check the time (or start a chronometer on your watch to count the minutes), and check the time after every few questions to make sure you are "on schedule."

If you are forced to speed up, do it efficiently. Usually one or more answer choices can be eliminated without too much difficulty. Above all, don't panic. Don't speed up and just begin guessing at random choices. By pacing yourself, and continually monitoring your progress against your watch, you will always know exactly how far ahead or behind you are with your available time. If you find that you are one minute behind on the test, don't skip one question without spending any time on it, just to catch back up. Take 15 fewer seconds on the next four questions, and after four questions you'll have caught back up. Once you catch back up, you can continue working each problem at your normal pace.

Furthermore, don't dwell on the problems that you were rushed on. If a problem was taking up too much time and you made a hurried guess, it must be difficult. The difficult questions are the ones you are most likely to miss anyway, so it isn't a big loss. It is better to end with more time than you need than to run out of time.

Lastly, sometimes it is beneficial to slow down if you are constantly getting ahead of time. You are always more likely to catch a careless mistake by working more slowly than quickly, and among very high-scoring test takers (those who are likely to have lots of time left over), careless errors affect the score more than mastery of material.

Secret Key #2 - Guessing is not Guesswork

You probably know that guessing is a good idea - unlike other standardized tests, there is no penalty for getting a wrong answer. Even if you have no idea about a question, you still have a 20-25% chance of getting it right.

Most test takers do not understand the impact that proper guessing can have on their score. Unless you score extremely high, guessing will significantly contribute to your final score.

Monkeys Take the Test

What most test takers don't realize is that to insure that 20-25% chance, you have to guess randomly. If you put 20 monkeys in a room to take this test, assuming they answered once per question and behaved themselves, on average they would get 20-25% of the questions correct. Put 20 test takers in the room, and the average will be much lower among guessed questions. Why?

1. The test writers intentionally writes deceptive answer choices that "look" right. A test taker has no idea about a question, so picks the "best looking" answer, which is often wrong. The monkey has no idea what looks good and what doesn't, so will consistently be lucky about 20-25% of the time.

2. Test takers will eliminate answer choices from the guessing pool based on a hunch or intuition. Simple but correct answers often get excluded, leaving a 0% chance of being correct. The monkey has no clue, and often gets lucky with the best choice.

This is why the process of elimination endorsed by most test courses is flawed and detrimental to your performance- test takers don't guess, they make an ignorant stab in the dark that is usually worse than random.

$5 Challenge

Let me introduce one of the most valuable ideas of this course- the $5 challenge:

You only mark your "best guess" if you are willing to bet $5 on it.

You only eliminate choices from guessing if you are willing to bet $5 on it.

Why $5? Five dollars is an amount of money that is small yet not insignificant, and can really add up fast (20 questions could cost you $100). Likewise, each answer choice on one question of the test will have a small impact on your overall score, but it can really add up to a lot of points in the end.

The process of elimination IS valuable. The following shows your chance of guessing it right:

If you eliminate wrong answer choices until only this many remain:	1	2	3
Chance of getting it correct:	100%	50%	33%

However, if you accidentally eliminate the right answer or go on a hunch for an incorrect answer, your chances drop dramatically: to 0%. By guessing among all the answer choices, you are GUARANTEED to have a shot at the right answer.

That's why the $5 test is so valuable- if you give up the advantage and safety of a pure guess, it had better be worth the risk.

What we still haven't covered is how to be sure that whatever guess you make is truly random. Here's the easiest way:

Always pick the first answer choice among those remaining.

Such a technique means that you have decided, **before you see a single test question**, exactly how you are going to guess- and since the order of choices tells you nothing about which one is correct, this guessing technique is perfectly random.

This section is not meant to scare you away from making educated guesses or eliminating choices- you just need to define when a choice is worth eliminating. The $5 test, along with a pre-defined random guessing strategy, is the best way to make sure you reap all of the benefits of guessing.

Secret Key #3 - Practice Smarter, Not Harder

Many test takers delay the test preparation process because they dread the awful amounts of practice time they think necessary to succeed on the test. We have refined an effective method that will take you only a fraction of the time.

There are a number of "obstacles" in your way to succeed. Among these are answering questions, finishing in time, and mastering test-taking strategies. All must be executed on the day of the test at peak performance, or your score will suffer. The test is a mental marathon that has a large impact on your future.

Just like a marathon runner, it is important to work your way up to the full challenge. So first you just worry about questions, and then time, and finally strategy:

Success Strategy

1. Find a good source for practice tests.
2. If you are willing to make a larger time investment, consider using more than one study guide- often the different approaches of multiple authors will help you "get" difficult concepts.
3. Take a practice test with no time constraints, with all study helps "open book." Take your time with questions and focus on applying strategies.
4. Take a practice test with time constraints, with all guides "open book."
5. Take a final practice test with no open material and time limits

If you have time to take more practice tests, just repeat step 5. By gradually exposing yourself to the full rigors of the test environment, you will condition your mind to the stress of test day and maximize your success.

Secret Key #4 - Prepare, Don't Procrastinate

Let me state an obvious fact: if you take the test three times, you will get three different scores. This is due to the way you feel on test day, the level of preparedness you have, and, despite the test writers' claims to the contrary, some tests WILL be easier for you than others.

Since your future depends so much on your score, you should maximize your chances of success. In order to maximize the likelihood of success, you've got to prepare in advance. This means taking practice tests and spending time learning the information and test taking strategies you will need to succeed.

Never take the test as a "practice" test, expecting that you can just take it again if you need to. Feel free to take sample tests on your own, but when you go to take the official test, be prepared, be focused, and do your best the first time!

Secret Key #5 - Test Yourself

Everyone knows that time is money. There is no need to spend too much of your time or too little of your time preparing for the test. You should only spend as much of your precious time preparing as is necessary for you to get the score you need.

Once you have taken a practice test under real conditions of time constraints, then you will know if you are ready for the test or not.

If you have scored extremely high the first time that you take the practice test, then there is not much point in spending countless hours studying. You are already there.

Benchmark your abilities by retaking practice tests and seeing how much you have improved. Once you score high enough to guarantee success, then you are ready.

If you have scored well below where you need, then knuckle down and begin studying in earnest. Check your improvement regularly through the use of practice tests under real conditions. Above all, don't worry, panic, or give up. The key is perseverance!

Then, when you go to take the test, remain confident and remember how well you did on the practice tests. If you can score high enough on a practice test, then you can do the same on the real thing.

General Strategies

The most important thing you can do is to ignore your fears and jump into the test immediately- do not be overwhelmed by any strange-sounding terms. You have to jump into the test like jumping into a pool- all at once is the easiest way.

Make Predictions

As you read and understand the question, try to guess what the answer will be. Remember that several of the answer choices are wrong, and once you begin reading them, your mind will immediately become cluttered with answer choices designed to throw you off. Your mind is typically the most focused immediately after you have read the question and digested its contents. If you can, try to predict what the correct answer will be. You may be surprised at what you can predict.

Quickly scan the choices and see if your prediction is in the listed answer choices. If it is, then you can be quite confident that you have the right answer. It still won't hurt to check the other answer choices, but most of the time, you've got it!

Answer the Question

It may seem obvious to only pick answer choices that answer the question, but the test writers can create some excellent answer choices that are wrong. Don't pick an answer just because it sounds right, or you believe it to be true. It MUST answer the question. Once you've made your selection, always go back and check it against the question and make sure that you didn't misread the question, and the answer choice does answer the question posed.

Benchmark

After you read the first answer choice, decide if you think it sounds correct or not. If it doesn't, move on to the next answer choice. If it does, mentally mark that answer choice. This doesn't mean that you've definitely selected it as your answer choice, it just means that it's the best you've seen thus far. Go ahead and read the next choice. If the next choice is worse than the one you've already selected, keep going to the next answer choice. If the next choice is better than the choice you've already selected, mentally mark the new answer choice as your best guess.

The first answer choice that you select becomes your standard. Every other answer choice must be benchmarked against that standard. That choice is correct until proven otherwise by another answer choice beating it out. Once you've decided that no other answer choice seems as good, do one final check to ensure that your answer choice answers the question posed.

Valid Information

Don't discount any of the information provided in the question. Every piece of information may be necessary to determine the correct answer. None of the information in the question is there to throw you off (while the answer choices will certainly have information to throw you off). If two seemingly unrelated topics are discussed, don't ignore either. You can be confident there is a relationship, or it wouldn't be included in the question, and you are probably going to have to determine what is that relationship to find the answer.

Avoid "Fact Traps"

Don't get distracted by a choice that is factually true. Your search is for the answer that answers the question. Stay focused and don't fall for an answer that is true but incorrect. Always go back to the question and make sure you're choosing an answer that actually answers the question and is not just a true statement. An answer can be factually correct, but it MUST answer the question asked. Additionally, two answers can both be seemingly correct, so be sure to read all of the answer choices, and make sure that you get the one that BEST answers the question.

Milk the Question

Some of the questions may throw you completely off. They might deal with a subject you have not been exposed to, or one that you haven't reviewed in years. While your lack of knowledge about the subject will be a hindrance, the question itself can give you many clues that will help you find the correct answer. Read the question carefully and look for clues. Watch particularly for adjectives and nouns describing difficult terms or words that you don't recognize. Regardless of if you completely understand a word or not, replacing it with a synonym either provided or one you more familiar with may help you to understand what the questions are asking. Rather than wracking your mind about specific detailed information concerning a difficult term or word, try to use mental substitutes that are easier to understand.

The Trap of Familiarity

Don't just choose a word because you recognize it. On difficult questions, you may not recognize a number of words in the answer choices. The test writers don't put "make-believe" words on the test; so don't think that just because you only recognize all the words in one answer choice means that answer choice must be correct. If you only recognize words in one answer choice, then focus on that one. Is it correct? Try your best to determine if it is correct. If it is, that is great, but if it doesn't, eliminate it. Each word and answer choice you eliminate increases your chances of getting the question correct, even if you then have to guess among the unfamiliar choices.

Eliminate Answers

Eliminate choices as soon as you realize they are wrong. But be careful! Make sure you consider all of the possible answer choices. Just because one appears right, doesn't mean that the next one won't be even better! The test writers will usually put more than one good answer choice for every question, so read all of them. Don't worry if you are stuck between two that seem right. By getting down to just two remaining possible choices, your odds are now 50/50. Rather than wasting too much time, play the odds. You are guessing, but guessing wisely, because you've been able to knock out some of the answer choices that you know are wrong. If you are eliminating choices and realize that the last answer choice you are left with is also obviously wrong, don't panic. Start over and consider each choice again. There may easily be something that you missed the first time and will realize on the second pass.

Tough Questions

If you are stumped on a problem or it appears too hard or too difficult, don't waste time. Move on! Remember though, if you can quickly check for obviously incorrect answer choices, your chances of guessing correctly are greatly improved. Before you completely give up, at least try to knock out a couple of possible answers. Eliminate what you can and then guess at the remaining answer choices before moving on.

Brainstorm

If you get stuck on a difficult question, spend a few seconds quickly brainstorming. Run through the complete list of possible answer choices. Look at each choice and ask yourself, "Could this answer the question satisfactorily?" Go through each answer choice and consider it independently of the other. By systematically going through all possibilities, you may find something that you would otherwise overlook. Remember that when you get stuck, it's important to try to keep moving.

Read Carefully

Understand the problem. Read the question and answer choices carefully. Don't miss the question because you misread the terms. You have plenty of time to read each question thoroughly and make sure you understand what is being asked. Yet a happy medium must be attained, so don't waste too much time. You must read carefully, but efficiently.

Face Value

When in doubt, use common sense. Always accept the situation in the problem at face value. Don't read too much into it. These problems will not require you to make huge leaps of logic. The test writers aren't trying to throw you off with a cheap trick. If you have to go beyond creativity and make a leap of logic in order to have an answer choice answer the question, then you should look at the other answer choices. Don't overcomplicate the problem by creating theoretical relationships or explanations that will warp time or space. These are normal problems rooted in reality. It's just that the applicable relationship or explanation may not be readily apparent and you have to figure things out. Use your common sense to interpret anything that isn't clear.

Prefixes

If you're having trouble with a word in the question or answer choices, try dissecting it. Take advantage of every clue that the word might include. Prefixes and suffixes can be a huge help. Usually they allow you to determine a basic meaning. Pre- means before, post- means after, pro - is positive, de- is negative. From these prefixes and suffixes, you can get an idea of the general meaning of the word and try to put it into context. Beware though of any traps. Just because con is the opposite of pro, doesn't necessarily mean congress is the opposite of progress!

Hedge Phrases

Watch out for critical "hedge" phrases, such as likely, may, can, will often, sometimes, often, almost, mostly, usually, generally, rarely, sometimes. Question writers insert these hedge phrases to cover every possibility. Often an answer choice will be wrong simply because it leaves no room for exception. Avoid answer choices that have definitive words like "exactly," and "always".

Switchback Words

Stay alert for "switchbacks". These are the words and phrases frequently used to alert you to shifts in thought. The most common switchback word is "but". Others include although, however, nevertheless, on the other hand, even though, while, in spite of, despite, regardless of.

New Information

Correct answer choices will rarely have completely new information included. Answer choices typically are straightforward reflections of the material asked about and will directly relate to the question. If a new piece of information is included in an answer choice that doesn't even seem to relate to the topic being asked about, then that answer choice is likely incorrect. All of the information needed to answer the question is usually provided for you, and so you should not have to make guesses that are unsupported or choose answer choices that require unknown information that cannot be reasoned on its own.

Time Management

On technical questions, don't get lost on the technical terms. Don't spend too much time on any one question. If you don't know what a term means, then since you don't have a dictionary, odds are you aren't going to get much further. You should immediately recognize terms as whether or not you know them. If you don't, work with the other clues that you have, the other answer choices and terms provided, but don't waste too much time trying to figure out a difficult term.

Contextual Clues

Look for contextual clues. An answer can be right but not correct. The contextual clues will help you find the answer that is most right and is correct. Understand the context in which a phrase or statement is made. This will help you make important distinctions.

Don't Panic

Panicking will not answer any questions for you. Therefore, it isn't helpful. When you first see the question, if your mind goes blank, take a deep breath. Force yourself to mechanically go through the steps of solving the problem and using the strategies you've learned.

Pace Yourself

Don't get clock fever. It's easy to be overwhelmed when you're looking at a page full of questions, your mind is full of random thoughts and feeling confused, and the clock is ticking down faster than you would like. Calm down and maintain the pace that you have set for yourself. As long as you are on track by monitoring your pace, you are guaranteed to have enough time for yourself. When you get to the last few minutes of the test, it may seem like you won't have enough time left, but if you only have as many questions as you should have left at that point, then you're right on track!

Answer Selection

The best way to pick an answer choice is to eliminate all of those that are wrong, until only one is left and confirm that is the correct answer. Sometimes though, an answer choice may immediately look right. Be careful! Take a second to make sure that the other choices are not equally obvious. Don't make a hasty mistake. There are only two times that you should stop before checking other answers. First is when you are positive that the answer choice you have selected is correct. Second is when time is almost out and you have to make a quick guess!

Check Your Work

Since you will probably not know every term listed and the answer to every question, it is important that you get credit for the ones that you do know. Don't miss any questions through careless mistakes. If at all possible, try to take a second to look back over your answer selection and make sure you've selected the correct answer choice and haven't made a costly careless mistake (such as marking an answer choice that you didn't mean to mark). This quick double check should more than pay for itself in caught mistakes for the time it costs.

Beware of Directly Quoted Answers

Sometimes an answer choice will repeat word for word a portion of the question or reference section. However, beware of such exact duplication – it may be a trap! More than likely, the correct choice will paraphrase or summarize a point, rather than being exactly the same wording.

Slang

Scientific sounding answers are better than slang ones. An answer choice that begins "To compare the outcomes..." is much more likely to be correct than one that begins "Because some people insisted..."

Extreme Statements

Avoid wild answers that throw out highly controversial ideas that are proclaimed as established fact. An answer choice that states the "process should be used in certain situations, if..." is much more likely to be correct than one that states the "process should be discontinued completely." The first is a calm rational statement and doesn't even make a definitive, uncompromising stance, using a hedge word "if" to provide wiggle room, whereas the second choice is a radical idea and far more extreme.

Answer Choice Families

When you have two or more answer choices that are direct opposites or parallels, one of them is usually the correct answer. For instance, if one answer choice states "x increases" and another answer choice states "x decreases" or "y increases," then those two or three answer choices are very similar in construction and fall into the same family of answer choices. A family of answer choices is when two or three answer choices are very similar in construction, and yet often have a directly opposite meaning. Usually the correct answer choice will be in that family of answer choices. The "odd man out" or answer choice that doesn't seem to fit the parallel construction of the other answer choices is more likely to be incorrect.

Special Report: Additional Bonus Material

Due to our efforts to try to keep this book to a manageable length, we've created a link that will give you access to all of your additional bonus material.

Please visit http://www.mometrix.com/bonus948/cgfm3gfmc to access the information.